BEATING THE ODDS

A practical guide to navigating sexism in Australian universities

MARCIA DEVLIN

Disclaimer

The material in this publication is of the nature of general comment only and does not represent professional advice. It is not intended to provide specific guidance for any particular circumstances, and it should not be relied upon for any decision to take action or not to take action on any matter that it covers. Readers should obtain professional advice where appropriate, before making any such decision. To the maximum extent permitted by law, the author and publisher disclaim all responsibility and liability to any person, arising directly or indirectly from any person taking or not taking action based on the information in this book.

ISBN: 978-0-6451010-3-4

First published May 2021 by Marcia Devlin
57 Erskine St, North Melbourne, Victoria, 3051
Reprinted August 2021

© **Marcia Devlin, 2021**

The moral rights of the author have been asserted.

All rights reserved. Except as permitted under the *Australian Copyright Act 1968* (for example, a fair dealing for the purposes of study, research, criticism or review), no part of this book may be reproduced, stored in a retrieval system, communicated or transmitted in any form or by any means without prior written permission. All inquiries should be made to the publisher at the above address.

Cover design and inside pages by Claire McGregor, Kookaburra Hill Publishing Services.

To Pete.
For all the things.

Contents

Foreword	vii
Introduction	1
CHAPTER ONE **The Odds Are Against You**	9
CHAPTER TWO **You're Expected to Be a Good Girl**	31
CHAPTER THREE **Get an Attitude**	49
CHAPTER FOUR **Prepare a Secret Strategy**	71
CHAPTER FIVE **Do More of What Counts – and Less of What Doesn't**	91
CHAPTER SIX **Form a Support Squad**	123
CHAPTER SEVEN **Beating the Odds**	149
References	171
Acknowledgements	175
About the Author	177

Foreword

The red moon of 2018 was the global shift into what Indigenous people call 'Grandmother Time'. Some call it 'eighth fire', or 'seventh generation'. This marks the start of 100 years of female-led energy for the world.

Women leaders will emerge with ancient wisdom, vitality, and a unique approach that honours their male energy and calls on their female energy.

This also marks the time in which men recognise their female energy within and acquiesce to it, feeling deep relief and allowing this energy to rise.

As a botanist would say, a plant that holds both sexes is known as 'perfect'. Humans hold both male and female energy, and female leadership in Grandmother Time speaks to those dual energies, leading thinking, decisions, behaviour and actions.

It is the time for what the Algonquian peoples near the Rocky Mountains call 'caucus' decision-making, where every voice is heard and valued equally as holding both male and female energy.

It is the time when we are going to be humbled by the world which we cannot control. It is a time to be reminded to act in sync with the world, in partnership – more eco and less ego.

It is the time to recognise female energy in leadership is a tremendous gift to us all.

Marcia Devlin's book is the ideal conduit for the energy of Grandmother Time, calling on universities and those in power to embrace female leadership and to imagine and create new ways of leading from within.

More importantly, Marcia's brilliant book is witty and wise, demonstrating the power of vulnerability for victory.

This book is an example of true strength and the female energy of taking what hurts us, harms us, and at times feels like it may diminish us, and using it to expand our potency in smart and intelligent ways.

Marcia says, 'it won't happen overnight, but it will happen'.

Aboriginal philosophy tells us that female leadership is inevitable.

Arabella Douglas Gnibi
Minyunbal Woman

Introduction

This book is for ambitious women

I started writing this book primarily for academic women in Australian universities. I've been an Australian academic for 30 years and I understand your world. I've been a woman for longer than that, and I understand what being a woman – and the subject of sexism – means for a career in Australian universities.

As I started to write, I realised most of the book is relevant to women who work in universities in professional and so-called 'third space' roles as well. If this is you, you can just use Chapter One as context and skim-read the bits of Chapter Five that are specifically about teaching and research. The rest of the book is applicable to your role and situation. Hello and welcome.

Most of the book is also relevant to women in management and leadership in universities, so hello to you too, whether you're in academic or professional roles.

Friends outside of academia have found much of the content of the book is relevant to women in other workplaces similar to universities, including TAFE colleges, polytechnics, private providers, and government departments and agencies. Welcome to you too.

If you're reading this book and you think it has ideas that are useful for women, or men, please feel free to buy a copy for every woman or man you know. Christmas is coming. Or Easter. One of them is always coming. And presents are nice.

This is not an academic book

If you are looking for a research-heavy book, based on data from formal interviews undertaken within an ethics-approved research framework, the contents of which have been transcribed, then thematically analysed within academic theory and written up with reference to the body of relevant international literature, with lots of citations, put this book back on the shelf now. Proceed immediately to your nearest university library to find the tome you are seeking – this is not it.

This is a rigorous book

Claims are made and evidence is supplied to back them up. Some of the evidence is from government statistics. Some of the evidence is from me hand-counting how many female chancellors and vice-chancellors we have in Australia (spoiler alert: not enough – see Chapter One). Most of the evidence in the book is from women's stories, shared and gathered over the three decades I have worked in universities. There are probably fancy names for the mixed methods I've used, but I haven't worried about that in this book.

This is a plain-speaking, down-to-earth, practical book, mostly free of paradigms, theories, academic jargon and the like. I do mention one theory in Chapter Two. The book has relatively few references, except where it is simply not possible to avoid giving a nod to the person whose idea I am including. But I have kept such inclusion to a minimum. I have listed sources I do use at the end of the book, so you can check my claims. There are a small number of footnotes – these are mainly to accommodate my tangential thinking from time to time.

I have tried to write something easy to read, honest and, most of all, useful to women working in universities and similar organisations. I've based the contents on: stuff I've seen, experienced and thought about over my 30 years in academia; conversations with scores of senior women; and supervising, mentoring, sponsoring and interacting with hundreds, if not thousands, of women in that time.

This book is not about sexual harassment or assault

This book is not about sexual harassment or sexual assault of women in universities (although there is one anecdote in Chapter Seven before which I give a trigger warning, so you can avoid the anecdote if you want or need to). Partly because of their complexity and sensitivity, I have largely chosen to steer clear of those topics in this book. But I'd hate you to think I don't know these behaviours go on, or to think I don't care about them. I know they go on. I have experienced them, as have more than half the women I know. Some of the stories are shocking, others heartbreaking. Writing about them is another book.

This book is about navigating sexism

This book is a candid account of the things that plague women in academia who wish to be successful, whether they aim to advance to professorial appointments and/or to positions of leadership or not. This book is about sexism. It offers, for your consideration, some of the strategies that some of us who've made it up quite high have found useful to getting and staying there, while remaining relatively sane and healthy. There is no one solution to the systemic, long-standing issues we face as women. And not all I suggest in here will work for everyone – we're all different and we're all on individual journeys through academia and life. But hopefully you will find something of value (and if you do, you will recommend the book to others, so I can become a febillionnaire* from book sales and retire).

I have written this book for three reasons

First, I find writing therapeutic, and after surviving 30 years in universities as a woman, including eight years as an executive where the majority of my colleagues were men, I needed some therapy.

But you need to know I am not a man-hater. In fact, I love men. I am very happily married to one and have been for a long time. We have two young adult sons. I adore these three men and everything about them. My four best friends from school and university are all men. I love them too. They all live interstate but I speak to one of them almost weekly and the other three at least annually. My favourite colleague from the most recent university executive team I served on is a man. My primary mentor is a man. Have I convinced you I love men? Good. I do. But you might feel I don't love them when you read some of what I have written in this book.

Second, I want to help women coming up behind me, which has always given me enormous satisfaction and joy. Having mentored and coached so many women over so many years, I have honed the messages all women in

---

* This is a name I just made up for a female billionaire. I like the sound of this. (There's a little bit of this sort of nonsense in the book.)

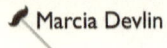
Marcia Devlin

universities and similar organisations would benefit from hearing and put them into this book. And there is only so much I can do one to one – my goal with a book is to get these messages out to more women in a resource-effective way.

Third, I am writing this book so I can become a bestselling author and febillionnaire, like all writers. Oh, wait... *checks notes* it seems writers don't make any money, so just as well I have the first two reasons.

Who am I?

Why should you care what I say? What would I know? And who am I anyway?

I made it to the top of academia and to the second top of senior executive. In 1990, my first real job after university was as an administrative assistant in a university department. My academic career started in 1991 as a tutor. I have since been a sessional, lecturer, senior lecturer, associate professor, professor, deputy director, director, executive director, honorary professor, adjunct professor, deputy vice-chancellor, senior deputy vice-chancellor and senior vice-president, but not in that order. I have worked in eight universities if I don't double-count the ones that merged and changed names or double-count the ones I have worked at, left and gone back to later. I have consulted to, and provided professional development programs for, numerous other universities. Most of my work has been in Australia, but I have also worked at universities overseas for short periods, including in Hong Kong and the United Kingdom. I serve on a number of editorial, advisory and company boards.

I am a leading researcher. I am recognised nationally and internationally for my evidence-based expertise in education and equity. I am an elected Lifelong Fellow of the Society for Research in Higher Education in the United Kingdom. With colleagues, I have won over $AUD6 million in external competitive research, project and other funds. I am frequently commissioned by government, universities, education providers and professional associations to undertake research and to produce outputs including policy and other advice – to improve education and address inequality.

I am well published. I have over 320 publications comprising academic and non-academic outputs. I currently write invited quarterly policy columns for the Higher Education Research Society of Australia and the Society for Research in Higher Education. My work is widely read and cited. I have a strong media profile, having written for APN Educational Media and Fairfax Media for over 20 years each. I had a commissioned column with Fairfax for 13 years.

I am a sought-after speaker. I have given over 100 keynote and other invited addresses in 10 countries. I have been invited to speak at Australian Women's Leadership Symposiums, Women in Higher Education Leadership Summits, the WATTLE Women Attaining Leadership Program, and Women in STEM, among many other female-focused events.

I am an award-winning leader. I have won several national and state leadership awards and was a state finalist for the Telstra Business Women's Award. In 2020, *The Educator* placed me on the 'hot list' of the top 50 educators in higher education in Australia. That's the only hot list I've ever been on (nerds bloom late). From 2017–2019, I was the elected national co-chair of Universities Australia Executive Women – an initiative of the peak body Universities Australia to work strategically to increase the number and proportion of women in leadership in Australian universities. During my time as co-chair, I co-commissioned and co-produced a widely read guide on recruiting more women into senior roles in universities and another on sponsorship of women.

That's the fancy bio. Hopefully, it convinces you I have done some stuff and know some stuff. And that I care about the advancement of women in universities.

Here's some less fancy, but arguably more relevant, stuff.

I have formally and informally coached and mentored hundreds of women working in universities. I have created and introduced two university-wide programs designed to mentor women at scale and provide peer support and development. I have supported countless women to win awards – for their teaching, their leadership, their policy-making and their administration. Women have told me I have inspired them to ask for raises, say no to unfair requests, query decisions that negatively affect their career, make enquiries about pay gaps, challenge biases, negotiate higher salaries, change jobs, support their daughters in their ambitions, enrol in further qualifications to improve their career options and to improve their sense of worth and self-esteem. These achievements are among those I am most proud of across my career.

The bios above are written to emphasise my successes and achievements – and don't mention the multiple failures and myriad of disasters that have also been a part of my career. Social media has encouraged us to believe that including the catastrophic bits is not advisable. That me including my catastrophic bits won't help me promote a book about how to succeed in academia. I beg to differ. I think being honest about these bits will help you, so I mention some of them in the book.

In summary, I've been around a while and made it to the highest echelons of academia, *and I'm a woman*. The data will show you can't get up that high easily if you are female. I have useful insights to offer for your consideration. There are trends and patterns in the experiences of academic and professional women I can point to. There are strategies women use that are more or less useful in various circumstances that you might benefit from knowing about. And there is comfort in knowing you are not alone by hearing the stories and insights of others. So those stories and insights are what I've filled the book with.

What women say about what is in this book

When I have previously shared material in this book in keynote and other invited presentations and workshops, female audience members usually give me feedback that falls into four broad categories.

The first is they find bits of my presentation depressing. Some of the facts, figures and stories I present make them feel hopeless and despondent. The second is they appreciate my candour about the ugly bits of some women's journeys. Hearing these accounts allows the women who have hit bumps in their journey to feel they are not alone and to begin to see that perhaps they are not the problem. And the ugly bits alert those who hadn't yet met obstacles to expect and prepare for them. The third category of feedback I regularly receive is that women find aspects of what I share inspiring. And the fourth is that I am funny.

I suspect you will find parts of this book depressing, other parts will validate your experience (or, if not, a pre-warning of bad stuff that might happen to you) and – I sincerely hope – you will find some parts inspiring. Hopefully, I will make you laugh at one point or another. But you might need to persist to get through the depressing bits to get to the validating/preparatory and inspiring bits. You'll be OK – I'll be here with you all the way through.

As a woman, the odds of succeeding in an Australian university are against you. And you are expected to accept this, like a good girl. If you don't want to accept this like a good girl, this book will help you get an attitude, prepare a secret strategy for your advancement, do more of what counts and less of what doesn't, form a top-notch support squad and successfully navigate the sexism of your workplace.

This book will help you to beat the odds.

Humour warning

Despite discussing serious issues – including sexism, inequality and unethical and other sorts of bad behaviour, as I mention above – there is a bit of humour in the book. I have deliberately chosen to use an irreverent tone and to take a humorous approach at times. This may seem incongruous to you, but I have always found humour to be one of the most useful tools in managing serious issues. I didn't think I could survive writing a whole book about a topic as serious as sexism without being silly or taking the proverbial, so I decided to just go with that flow and do what comes naturally.

I hope you enjoy it.

CHAPTER ONE

The Odds Are Against You

The good, the bad and the ugly

While the evidence shows there is a long way to go in achieving gender equity in universities, more women make it to the level of professor and take up senior roles in universities than was the case 10 years ago. It is likely that, with growing awareness and continued individual and cumulative effort, the trend toward greater gender equality will continue. That's some of the good news.

That said, if you want to advance in your academic career in Australia and you're a woman, the simple fact is: the odds are against you. The data show you are far less likely to advance to the top of the academic hierarchy than if you were a man. More likely, you'll be in the majority of women concentrated at the lower levels of academia. The data also show that most of the senior leadership roles in universities are held by men. So, as well as being less likely to make it to professor, you're also less likely to obtain a university senior leadership position. I'll show you the figures shortly. That's some of the bad news.

Sexism is, and stubbornly remains, an ingrained problem in Australian universities. The experiences of sexism women in Australian universities face are shocking, and the anecdotes and data show that these experiences have a detrimental cumulative effect on women's wellbeing and careers. While change is evident, it is small and incremental. It's not likely that gender inequity will be resolved easily or any time soon. That's the ugly news.

I'm sorry that in 2021 a book such as this one is necessary. The data doesn't lie – the forces working against women are strong. And change is hard. The situation appears grim. It's all a bit depressing, but, if you want

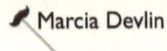
Marcia Devlin

to beat the odds, it will help to know what the odds are as a starting point. I'll lay out the figures and odds in this chapter. I've laid out the truth deliberately to ensure you understand the set of challenges before you as a woman, which you may not have been aware of, and to show you the scale of these challenges.

> *Sexism is, and stubbornly remains, an ingrained problem in Australian universities.*

I want to motivate you to consider the advice that's offered, which you may not think is necessary if you don't understand the obstacles you are facing. I confess that I will try to make you a bit cross in this chapter, and the next, as a source of motivation. You need to pay close attention to the evidence I will present, consider this evidence carefully and then make some decisions about how you will use this knowledge and understanding. I'll come back to what to do about the situation you find yourself in later in the book. For now, get a cup of tea/glass of wine/Scotch on the rocks and prepare to be shocked (but maybe not surprised).

Where women reside across academic levels

Women dominate the lower levels of academia in Australia, with more women than men as associate lecturers (Level A) and lecturers (Level B). Conversely, men dominate the upper levels of academia, with more men than women as senior lecturers (Level C), associate professors (Level D) and professors (Level E). If you don't know this, then you might assume that by working hard and being a good academic citizen, success will follow. If you are a woman, this is an erroneous assumption – the data does not lie[1].

In 2019 – from the most recent figures available at the time of writing – there were 125,787 full-time and fractional full-time staff in Australian universities. Of course, I'm writing this in late 2020 and early 2021, when a global pandemic and massive purge of academic staff is underway across the Australian sector, following the closing of borders and subsequent drop in international student revenue. The figures will change. It will be interesting to see what the impact on numbers by gender will be, but for now, the 2019 figures are the most recent and accurate and make the point.

Of these 125,787 full-time staff, 54,204 were employed as academic staff members. We'll concentrate on those. Of these academic appointments, 28,572 (53 percent) were held by men and 25,632 (47 percent) were held by women. In one sense, men are already ahead – occupying more of the safer jobs compared to the casual workforce (or what a friend of a friend calls the 'pink collar workforce'). But, broadly speaking, the numbers and percentages of men and women are close to even, which makes what I'm about to tell you even more shocking. See Table 1.

Table 1: Number and percentage of full-time academic staff by gender, 2019

Female	Male	Total
25,632 (47%)	28,572 (53%)	54,204

Source: https://docs.education.gov.au/node/53179

In 2019, there were 9,519 full-time Level A academics in Australia – 4,426 (46.5 percent) male and 5,093 (53.5 percent) female. The proportions were relatively close, with females holding a slim majority of these positions (15 percent more women than men at Level A). See Table 2.

Table 2: Number and percentage of academic staff at Level A by gender, 2019

Female	Male	Difference
5,093 (53.5%)	4,426 (46.5%)	15% more women

Source: https://docs.education.gov.au/node/53179

At Level B, there were 16,681 full-time academics – 7,428 (44.5 percent) male and 9,253 (55.5 percent) female. Again, the proportions are relatively close, but again with women holding the majority of these positions (25 percent more women at Level B). See Table 3.

Table 3: Number and percentage of academic staff at Level B by gender, 2019

Female	Male	Difference
9,253 (55.5%)	7,428 (44.5%)	25% more women

Source: https://docs.education.gov.au/node/53179

The proportions start to favour men at Level C. In 2019, 12,079 staff were academics at senior lecturer level – 6,355 (53 percent) male and 5,724 (47 percent) female. From 25 percent more women at Level B, there is now a positive difference for men of 11 percent at Level C. See Table 4.

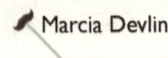
Marcia Devlin

Table 4: Number and percentage of academic staff at Level C by gender, 2019

Female	Male	Difference
5,724 (47%)	6,355 (53%)	11% more males

Source: https://docs.education.gov.au/node/53179

Levels D and E are reported together in the government statistics and are referred to here as the professoriate. Once we reach the professoriate, of the 15,925 full-time staff at this level, 10,363 (65 percent) are men, and just over half that number – 5,562 (35 percent) – are women. The percentage difference between men and women blows out remarkably in the professoriate – 86 percent more men at Levels D and E. See Table 5.

Table 5: Number and percentage of academic staff at Levels D and E by gender, 2019

Female	Male	Difference
5,562 (35%)	10,363 (65%)	86% more males

Source: https://docs.education.gov.au/node/53179

In summary, women are concentrated at the lower levels, and men dominate the highest level with 86 percent more men than women in the professoriate. If you think you're different in some way or other and getting stuck at the lower levels won't happen to you, you're both right and wrong. You are unique. But unless you proactively plan to navigate your way through your academic career, the odds are clear that you are less likely to advance in academia as a woman than if you were a man.

Is gender equity improving?

When we talk about the gender issues in Australian universities, we may hear the optimist's refrain, 'But things have improved!' They have, but let's have a look at the rate and the details of that improvement.

Comparing the 2019 professoriate figures to those from 10 years earlier gives us an indication of the extent that gender equity has improved. In 2009, there were 9,875 full-time academic staff in the professoriate – 7,257 (73.5 percent) men and 2,618 (26.5 percent) women. That is a 177 percent difference in favour of men. See Table 6.

Table 6: Number and percentage of academic staff at Levels D and E by gender, 2009 and 2019

2009		Difference	2019		Difference
Female	Male		Female	Male	
2,618 (26.5%)	7,257 (73.5%)	177% more males	5,562 (35%)	10,363 (65%)	86% more males

Source: https://docs.education.gov.au/node/53179

From 177 percent more males in the professoriate in 2009, there were 86 percent more males in the professoriate in 2019. Put another way, in the 10 years between 2009 and 2019, women have moved from being just over one-quarter of the professoriate to being just under one-third of the professoriate. That's certainly encouraging. See Table 7.

Table 7: Number and percentage of female academic staff at Levels D and E, 2009 and 2019

2009	2019	Difference
2,618 (26.5%)	5,562 (35%)	8.5% improvement for females

Source: https://docs.education.gov.au/node/53179

But look at the same figures in Table 7 again. In the 10 years between 2009 and 2019, women shifted from being 26.5 percent of the professoriate to being 35 percent – an upwards move of just 8.5 percent. If we keep going at this rate, then in another 10 years, in 2029, women will be 43.5 percent of the professoriate. Assuming the same rate is ongoing, all other things being equal, it will be the late-2030s before women make up half of the professoriate in Australian universities. That's almost 20 years from now. Are you comfortable with that?

Women in senior academic leadership

Given the state of the gender differences in academic levels, it is not surprising that the most senior academic appointment in a university, the vice-chancellor, is more often a man than a woman. At the time of writing this chapter in January 2021, of Australia's 37 public university vice-chancellors, 10 are women (27 percent) and 27 are men (73 percent). That's a percentage point difference of 50 percent and a percentage difference of – wait for it – 170 percent. There are 170 percent more male than female vice-chancellors

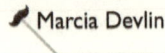
Marcia Devlin

in Australian public universities. Arguably, education is a traditionally female area, yet even in this sector, the majority – in this case around three-quarters – of the top jobs in Australia are held by men. See Table 8.

Table 8: Australian vice-chancellors by gender, January 2021

University	Female	Male
Australian Catholic University		√
Australian National University		√
Central Queensland University		√
Charles Darwin University		√
Charles Sturt University		√
Curtin University		√
Deakin University		√
Edith Cowan University		√
Federation University Australia		√
Flinders University		√
Griffith University	√	
James Cook University	√	
La Trobe University		√
Macquarie University		√
Monash University	√	
Murdoch University	√	
Queensland University of Technology	√	
RMIT University		√
Southern Cross University		√
Swinburne University of Technology	√	
University of Adelaide		√
University of Canberra		√
University of Melbourne		√
University of New England	√	
University of New South Wales		√
University of Newcastle		√
University of Queensland	√	
University of South Australia		√

University of Southern Queensland	√	
University of Sunshine Coast	√	
University of Sydney		√
University of Tasmania		√
University of Technology Sydney		√
University of Western Australia		√
University of Wollongong		√
Victoria University		√
Western Sydney University		√
TOTALS	**10 (27%)**	**27 (73%)**

Source: Australian university websites, January 2021.

The year 2020 was one of shifts in Australian university leadership, with vice-chancellors at 15 of the 37 public universities either announcing their departure from the top job or actually departing from the top job. The trends in the gender of new and incoming vice-chancellors to date are worth noting. As of January 2021, women had been appointed vice-chancellor in just four of the 15 interim or actual replacements made during 2020 (27 percent). In 11 of the 15 cases – 73 percent – a man won the role. See Table 9.

Table 9: Australian vice-chancellors appointed in 2020, by gender

University	Female	Male
Australian Catholic University		√
Charles Darwin University		√
Charles Sturt University		√
Curtin University		√
Federation University Australia		√
Southern Cross University		√
Swinburne University of Technology	√	
University of Adelaide		√
University of Canberra		√
University of Queensland	√	
University of Sunshine Coast	√	
University of Sydney		√
University of Western Australia		√

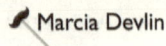
Marcia Devlin

University		
University of Wollongong	√	
Victoria University		√
TOTALS	**4 (27%)**	**11 (73%)**

Source: Australian university websites, January 2021.

This is a disappointing set of numbers. In the modern age, where it is widely known that women are just as competent as men, the opportunity for change inherent in 41 percent of the vice-chancellors in the country leaving their roles was not realised, with neither the number nor proportion of female vice-chancellors increasing.

In seven of the 15 cases where a replacement has been made to date, a male replaced a male vice-chancellor (47 percent). In four of the 15 cases, a male replaced a female (27 percent). In three of the cases, a female replaced a male (20 percent) and in the remaining case, a female replaced a female (7 percent). It is worth noting that two of the female appointees moved from one vice-chancellor position to another. Both were replaced by men in their former universities. See Table 10.

Table 10: Gender of incoming and outgoing Australian vice-chancellors as at January, 2021

University	Gender change			
	Male R* Male	Male R Female	Female R Male	Female R Female
Australian Catholic	√			
Charles Darwin	√			
Charles Sturt	√			
Curtin University		√		
Federation University		√		
Southern Cross		√		
Swinburne University				√
University of Adelaide	√			
University of Canberra	√			

* The R denotes 'replacing'. For example, Male R Male = a male replacing a male.

U of Queensland			√	
Sunshine Coast			√	
University of Sydney	√			
University of WA		√		
Wollongong			√	
Victoria University	√			
TOTALS	**7 (47%)**	**4 (27%)**	**3 (20%)**	**1 (7%)**

Source: Australian university websites, January 2021.

Admittedly, some of the male appointments are temporary while the formal recruitment processes are undertaken. But I'd suggest an incumbent man has more chance of winning the top gig than any un-incumbent woman. And of course the data shows a man is 170 percent more likely to get the job than a woman.

Women in chancellor positions

Chancellor positions in Australian universities are often operating less as the ceremonial position of olden days and more like the chair of the university board (also sometimes called the council or senate). Chancellors are increasingly responsible for leading not only the development of the university strategy but also for ensuring the smooth and successful running of the university as a business. These are key leadership roles on the Australian university landscape, with oversight of all aspects of a university. I'm sorry to have to tell you that the figures and proportions of women in chancellor leadership positions are similar to those of vice-chancellors.

At the time of writing in January 2021, just nine of the 37 public Australian university chancellors (24 percent) are women, which means 28 people (76 percent) in these top roles are men. In other words, there are 211 percent more male than female chancellors. On the positive side, the figures have improved in the last four years – when an organisation called *WomenCount*[2] checked in 2016, only 15 percent of chancellors were women. While a move from 15 to 24 percent female chancellors is positive, females still only make up less than one-quarter, and males make up a whopping more than three-quarters, of the people in these increasingly powerful roles. See Table 11.

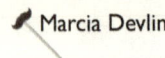

Table 11: Australian chancellors by gender, January 2021

University	Female	Male
Australian Catholic University		√
Australian National University	√	
Central Queensland University		√
Charles Darwin University		√
Charles Sturt University	√	
Curtin University		√
Deakin University		√
Edith Cowan University	√	
Federation University Australia		√
Flinders University		√
Griffith University		√
James Cook University		√
La Trobe University		√
Macquarie University		√
Monash University		√
Murdoch University		√
Queensland University of Technology	√	
RMIT University		√
Southern Cross University		√
Swinburne University of Technology		√
University of Adelaide	√	
University of Canberra		√
University of Melbourne		√
University of New England		√
University of New South Wales		√
University of Newcastle		√
University of Queensland		√
University of South Australia	√	
University of Southern Queensland		√
University of Sunshine Coast		√
University of Sydney	√	

University of Tasmania		√
University of Technology Sydney	√	
University of Western Australia		√
University of Wollongong	√	
Victoria University		√
Western Sydney University		√
TOTALS	9 (24%)	28 (76%)

Source: Australian university websites, January 2021.

In Victoria, Australia – where I live and which is home to eight universities – there are now no female chancellors. There was one – a temp for six months in late-2020 – but she's been replaced by a male. Three of the eight male Victorian chancellors are called John. So you're statistically more likely to become a chancellor in the state of Victoria if your name is John than if you are a woman.

Nationally, just one Australian university – Queensland University of Technology – has both a female vice-chancellor and a female chancellor at the same time. Of this group of 37 pairs of public university vice-chancellors and chancellors, less than three percent are both women. Conversely, the most frequent combination is – no surprise – a male chancellor paired with a male vice-chancellor, with 19 of 37 (51 percent) of public universities having that all-male power duo in place. See Table 12.

Table 12: Australian vice-chancellors and chancellors by gender, January 2021

University	VCs		Chancellors		Combined
	Female	Male	Female	Male	
Australian Catholic		√		√	MM
Australian National		√	√		
CQU		√		√	MM
Charles Darwin University		√		√	MM
Charles Sturt University		√	√		
Curtin University		√		√	MM
Deakin University		√		√	MM
Edith Cowan University		√	√		

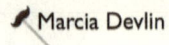
Marcia Devlin

University					
Federation University		√		√	MM
Flinders University		√		√	MM
Griffith University	√			√	
James Cook University	√			√	
La Trobe University		√		√	MM
Macquarie University		√		√	MM
Monash University	√			√	
Murdoch University	√			√	
QUT	√		√		FF
RMIT University		√		√	MM
Southern Cross University		√		√	MM
Swinburne	√			√	
University of Adelaide		√	√		
University of Canberra		√		√	MM
University of Melbourne		√		√	MM
University of New England	√			√	
UNSW		√		√	MM
University of Newcastle		√		√	MM
University of Queensland	√			√	
UniSA		√	√		
UQ	√			√	
Sunshine Coast	√			√	
University of Sydney		√	√		
University of Tasmania		√		√	MM
UTS		√	√		
UWA		√		√	MM
University of Wollongong		√	√		
Victoria University		√		√	MM
Western Sydney		√		√	MM

Source: Australian university websites, January 2021.

What are the odds?

Men hold 27 of the 37 vice-chancellor and 28 of the 37 chancellor roles in Australia – or 55 of the top 74 jobs. Women hold just 19 of these roles. The odds are, if you are a man, you are 189 percent more likely to hold one of the top two jobs as chancellor or vice-chancellor than if you are a woman. I don't know about you, but I find those odds pretty annoying. Why is this the case? Are women less intelligent or less capable than men? That's a rhetorical question, in case you're wondering.

At the risk of asking the obvious, why does this matter? While becoming the vice-chancellor is not everyone's academic career goal, one reason these data and facts matter is that the proportion of female vice-chancellors gives women in academia an indication of how likely it is they will rise to the very top of the organisation. Most vice-chancellors are professors, with two well-known (male) exceptions at the time of writing. There are fewer visible female role-models at the top of academia, and academic and university business leadership, than there are male role-models. Further, increasingly, councils – led by chancellors – make the decisions about the appointments of vice-chancellors (and sometimes have a say in deputy vice-chancellor appointments too). While men continue to dominate the decision-making in universities, there is unlikely to be the size and pace of change required to address the serious gender imbalance in leadership.

Why do men dominate in universities?

Women often blame themselves for their lack of advancement or their slow advancement. They think they haven't worked hard enough, or haven't been lucky enough, or aren't good enough to get promoted or be selected for leadership roles. Some women think they need to do more, or be more confident. But it's probably not entirely your fault you won't advance as easily as a man will advance. The reasons for the gender inequity are related to sexism, and I'll briefly outline these below. Chapter Two also looks at other possible reasons for inequity. These first two chapters provide the context for – and, hopefully, the motivation to consider – the practical suggestions in the second half of the book.

'Women have babies'

If you start asking questions about the gender imbalance in universities, you might find the person answering the question tips their head slightly to one side and says, 'Well, you see, women take time out to have babies.' They may make a helpless gesture with their hands at the same time. The implications

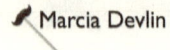
Marcia Devlin

are: the career interruption(s) to give birth impede academic and other progress *forever;* these are just the facts; the facts are self-explanatory; and there's not much anyone can do about this.

> *Gender inequity comes about, at least in part, because there are sexist views about women's role in society.*

While it might be true many women take time off to have and raise families, their actual absence is only for a relatively short period when a child is born. It's usually not decades that academic – or other – women are out of the workforce completely. Relatively short periods of time out does not, on its own, adequately explain career-long disadvantage. Children grow up, learn to dress and feed themselves, get where they need to be independently, and eventually move out. In many cases, women don't have children. But despite these facts, women as a cohort never catch up to men.

I am fully aware that only women can physically get pregnant and give birth. I have done this myself – twice. I am also aware that only women can breastfeed. I've breastfed children for more months than I care to count. (I also learnt how to express milk and put it in the fridge and, technically, a well-trained, supervised monkey could feed breastmilk to a baby from a bottle, but I digress). But apart from those wonderful, terrifying, amazing feats of the female body of giving birth and breastfeeding, there is no other biological reason that a woman has to be out of the workforce because she happened to give birth to and breastfeed one baby or more. Every other aspect of childcare and child raising, family and home creation – and, especially, housework – can be done equally well by the birth-giving woman and other people, including the other parent, relatives, friends and paid professionals.

Growing, birthing and breastfeeding babies (the bits of ensuring the continuation of the human race that women must do because men are not biologically capable of doing them) do not, *on their own*, explain why there are 86 percent more men than women in the academic professoriate in Australia, nor why around three-quarters of Australian vice-chancellors and chancellors are men. Arguing that the gender inequity in universities is because women give birth and breastfeed is nonsense and poppycock. Gender inequity comes about, at least in part, because there are sexist views about women's role in society.

Society is sexist

In trying to explain the gender inequity evident in universities, it is also argued that wider societal forces are at play. I have heard many times that the reason women are disadvantaged in universities is that they are disadvantaged more generally in society. I have heard more than once, 'Well, we live in a sexist world.' Often the comment is accompanied by the same helpless gesture I mentioned above. The implications are that:
- larger forces are at play in society;
- universities are part of that society;
- these are simply the facts;
- the facts are self-explanatory; and
- there's not much anyone can do about this.

Women are often expected to carry the heaviest loads in domestic spheres. This results in them having less time and energy for the attention and work required in academic and professional advancement. Housework is usually women's work, and this is true at home and at work in universities – I'll talk more about this, and what to do about it, later in the book. With the evolution of understanding and shifts underway in the advanced western economy of Australia, an increasing proportion of women have a split of family and domestic duties with their partners and outsourced help. That society is sexist and universities are part of society does not, on its own, explain an 86 percent gender difference in professorial appointments and a 170 percent gender difference in chancellor and vice-chancellor appointments.

University cultures and promotion processes favour men

I have coached and mentored scores of women in academia over more than two decades. Many of them have had children. It's a common theme among those who have had children that when they return from maternity leave, they have 'fallen behind'. Many return to work part-time while they juggle their paid job with their other (not insignificant and yet unpaid) job of keeping a mini-human or mini-humans alive. The gap in employment during the leave, sometimes coupled with the part-time status immediately afterwards, often means women lose traction with research and publishing. This loss of traction can be cumulative if you take more than one period of maternity leave and if you stay in a part-time capacity for a long period of time.

Many women have told me they return to heavy teaching loads, little or no internal support in the form of funding for research and little or no time

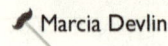
Marcia Devlin

release within their time fraction for research or publishing. One woman recently told me of her experience of returning to exactly these conditions. She watched men around her at the same level 'with a wife at home, taking care of the kids' move up the academic scales while she – working just as hard and feeling like she was working even harder – did not move 'for years and years'. Her work at the lower levels enabled the men to be 'freed up' from lower-level duties to pursue the activities that would help them advance.

Many women have told me they have watched men get more opportunities in leadership roles from male deans, and men are more often invited to join research grants of other men. They have also told me of feeling like they are working in a 'blokey' culture, where men are in charge and succeeding while women are playing the support roles. However, many women have also been overlooked and denied opportunities by senior women. This is particularly disappointing for those who understand the critical need for women to support each other in order to make the necessary changes.

Many universities are trying to address these issues. But after many years of sitting on and chairing academic promotion committees, I can see that, despite much goodwill and many good people doing their best, university systems of reward and recognition – and therefore, advancement – tend to favour men's relatively uninterrupted and neat career trajectories, greater freedom to engage in research and publishing, more easily quantified outputs and more frequent leadership opportunities.

Most universities have introduced some form of consideration of performance relative to opportunity in promotion processes. One woman told me recently she applied for promotion and, in her application, tried to make a strong case for consideration of performance relative to opportunity. She had evidence that, since returning from maternity leave, she had been given a heavy teaching load, no research funding support, no time release for research or publishing and had been offered no opportunity for leadership. Despite this, she had managed to achieve high teaching evaluations from students and advanced some research and scholarship in her own time – mostly unpaid. Her application was not successful. The feedback provided was her teaching was '10 out of 10' but she should 'stop whingeing' about a lack of research opportunities provided to her after maternity leave in her application. This, she was told, had 'made the panel feel uncomfortable'.

This same woman told me she had 'made a bit of noise' about the unfairness of the situation she faced on returning from maternity leave. She pointed out the support provided by other universities. She told me other women have since benefited from her agitation, but she herself did not. She was eventually promoted but feels she was stuck at lower levels for far too long and wishes that hadn't been the case. She also told me she wished she had known some of the advice I provide later in the book when she was fighting for her place in academia.

The truth is, some promotion panels struggle with these cases for equity and consideration of performance relative to opportunity. They agonise over giving what is seen as a possible advantage to someone who doesn't have the traditional, easily documented and easily counted runs on the board (i.e., grant dollars and high-status publications).

> *I sometimes wonder about the subtle but powerful impact of the language used in the culture of universities.*

In recent years I've started to see more men using this performance relative to opportunity mechanism to help themselves advance. A memorable recent case involved a man applying for promotion to associate professor, claiming a case for consideration of performance relative to opportunity. The reason for the claim was his wife had had a baby and the child woke up in the night a lot to be breastfed. Sometimes, he wrote, he himself got out of bed and brought the baby to his wife to feed. This, he argued, had disturbed his sleep and therefore becoming a father had negatively impacted on his research productivity. You can't make these things up. A female promotion panel colleague wryly suggested to me later that day in private that, as well as promoting him to the professoriate (as the panel did that day), we might also consider nominating him for a Father of the Year Award.

I sometimes wonder about the subtle but powerful impact of the language used in the culture of universities. For example, we have 'Bachelor' and 'Master' degrees and one can become a 'Fellow'. There are no Spinsters of Science or Mistresses of Engineering – and what's the gender variant for 'Fellow' anyway? While there are others with far superior knowledge about the impact of language on the world than I, the following anecdote makes a point about the part language plays in thinking – both inside and outside – universities.

A few years ago, I was on a board that provided scholarship opportunities for tertiary students. We were determining the process for appointing a new chair. During the discussion, one man on the board – let's call him Lou – referred to this position as 'chairman'. Some time into the discussion, irritated by the gender-exclusive language, I asked the sitting chair, whose name was Mark, whether we could adopt the term 'chair' rather than 'chairman' for the remainder of the discussion. Mark smiled and prepared to respond.

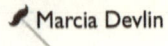
Marcia Devlin

Lou became quite animated. 'The correct term is chairman,' he interjected. I asked Lou, 'What if Kirsten becomes the chair? She's a woman so how can we call her a chairMAN?' He shot back, 'If Kirsten becomes the chairman, the correct term is Madam Chairman.' I couldn't resist. 'Well, Lou, the term 'woman' includes the term 'man' and so it can be used for both women and men. If Mark stays as chair, I'd like to suggest he be called 'SIR ChairWOMAN' from now on. 'SIR ChairWOMAN' is as sensible a term as the term 'Madam ChairMAN' you've just suggested for Kirsten.' Looking at the faces around the room, I was briefly concerned a number of board members might have a heart attack. The other two women on the board tried hard to hide their amusement. (Kirsten became the chair and was subsequently referred to as the 'Chair', not 'Madam Chairman'. Lou never spoke to me again.)

The people making the important decisions in universities are mostly men

Then there's the good, old-fashioned (literally) argument that women aren't advancing in academia because men make most of the important decisions. I can't help but wonder, after 30 years in the sector and meeting thousands of incredibly bright, ambitious and determined women, if there is sexist bias at play. Because most of the leaders and senior appointments are male, are they more likely to feel comfortable with other males near them at the top? I also wonder if there is resistance from some male leaders to welcoming women into the professoriate and into powerful senior leadership positions in universities. I also wonder whether the women who do make it to the top, consciously or otherwise, adopt some of the views and biases of men and therefore don't help with addressing the gender imbalance. Lots of wonderings. Just wonderings.

During a job search a few years ago, I received feedback that I missed out on being shortlisted for a senior role because 'other candidates had greater experience'. When the man who got the job was announced, I went straight to his LinkedIn profile and discovered he had about half the experience that I had. Later, I found out incorrect assumptions had been made about what he and I knew about a central component of the job. His knowledge had been overestimated and mine had been underestimated.

In my experience, this is quite common for women in academia and women looking for leadership opportunities in universities. Some argue it is due to unconscious gender bias where, for example, men are assumed to have potential, but women have to prove they have potential (which is a hard thing to prove – think about it). Whatever the reason, it's annoying and will likely play a part in your career journey, whether you know it yet or not.

Even when the women are in the upper echelons of Australian universities, there is often evidence of an 'old-school' way of doing things. I recently observed a (male) chancellor chairing a recruitment and selection panel for a senior executive position that would be reporting to the (female) vice-chancellor. I wondered why he – and not she – was chairing this panel. Surely, the extremely competent person appointed by council to lead the university could and should have chaired the panel? Certainly, she, like any vice-chancellor, could have benefited from the chancellor's input as a panel member, but ultimately why was she not the lead decision-maker about a position that would report to her? I marvelled at this vice-chancellor's remarkable tolerance and patience – these traits are probably part of the reason she has managed to make it to vice-chancellor, despite the odds.

With sexism, everyone's a loser

Sexism in Australian universities ultimately benefits no-one. Women, men and universities are missing out because of this sexism. Women miss out on higher-level jobs – and the privileges and opportunities that come with those roles and with achieving their unique potential. Men miss out on having talented female colleagues working alongside them as peers and equals. They don't get to hear views from perspectives different to their own. They don't get the opportunity to learn about things they may never have thought about previously. Universities miss out on the talent yet to be unleashed when more women lead, and on their subsequent contributions to meeting their objectives and missions, as well as their bottom lines.

Research highlighted by Adam Grant and Sheryl Sandberg in a 2014 *New York Times* article[3] shows when more women lead, organisational performance improves. The research studies they refer to show innovative organisations with more women in top management are more profitable, and companies with more gender diversity have more revenue, customers, market share and profits. While universities haven't traditionally measured themselves against these corporate metrics, universities are increasingly expected to run like companies and to focus on these sorts of metrics so they can better meet their education, research and community missions.

Not everyone has to be a loser because of sexism. I'm pretty sure you don't want to be a loser – and that's part of the reason you are reading this book. Keep reading – it gets worse in Chapter Two but then things definitely start to look up from Chapter Three onwards. I hope I can offer you strategies and ideas that will help you. I might even make you laugh.

Marcia Devlin

Can you beat the odds?

Whether because of childbirth, breastfeeding, time out of the workforce to raise families, time spent doing housework, societal forces, university culture and reward systems favouring men, or whatever other reason, there are more men at the top of Australian universities than women – and that's a fact. The odds of succeeding in academia are much lower for you, as a woman – another fact. No-one is shouting from the rooftops about this – yet another fact. This suggests we are, collectively, quite comfortable with the sexism and gender inequity we are all experiencing. Or perhaps we're too busy, tired and consumed by giving birth, breastfeeding, raising families, doing most of the housework, being smashed by societal forces, being annoyed about university cultures and reward systems favouring men, being irritated by being called a 'fellow' or 'Madam Chairman' and having all the decisions made by men, to do anything much about it. At least, not without some help.

You might think the odds don't apply to you because, for example, you don't have or don't want children. Or that you will be OK because you have a strong research track record already and this will stand you in good stead. Or because a senior person is sponsoring you (this is extremely rare, but good on you if you have a sponsor – you may well beat some of the odds). The data show, however – despite what you might think – that women just don't make it as easily as men in academia.

If you think gender discrimination doesn't apply to you, welcome to the club. I was oblivious to gender discrimination for much of my career. But then I started to have certain experiences, notice some trends and hear stories from other women. Now I have no doubt universities are inherently sexist places, but that is not to say every woman is discriminated against on the basis of gender every time. Some women – an increasing proportion – make it to the professoriate and to the very top of universities. Some senior male leaders – alongside many senior female leaders – are genuinely committed to and making efforts to address gender inequity. Things are slowly improving. They just may not improve quickly enough to address the disadvantage you are facing within the timespan of your career, unless you help things along.

In this book, I'm going to show you how to navigate the sexism that exists in Australian universities and advance your career in spite of it so you have a better chance of beating the odds. I can't guarantee you will beat them, but I can share some experiences, offer some advice and give you some suggestions so you can have a red-hot go.

Conclusion

You may find this chapter dispiriting or even depressing. The evidence is clear that, if you are a woman, the odds of succeeding in academia are against you. You are simply less likely to get to the professor level if you are a female academic. Using vice-chancellors and chancellors as proxy measures of women in leadership roles, your chances of becoming a leader in academia are also slimmer than they would be if you were a man.

Try not to feel discouraged by what is in this chapter. This book is here to help you feel hopeful about a career in academia. Unless you know about what is going on, and face up to it, you are at risk of drifting along at the lower levels for far too long. Things are getting better. Not that long ago, in the 1990s, one university I worked at only had toilets for women on every second floor in the main administration high-rise building – because why would you need any more female toilets than that? I am happy to report they now have women's toilets on every single floor of that same building. See? Hard evidence that things are improving.

If all else fails, you could always pretend to be a man. Inspired by American comedian Sarah Cooper[4], I wrote an article in 2016 about women in leadership while I was wearing a false moustache. Cooper's idea is if women wore these and, therefore, looked more like men, they'd get taken more seriously and be less threatening. My article got a lot of attention online, and when I republished it this year, the same thing happened. At a conference a year or so ago, some female colleagues and I donned false moustaches in a faux attempt to be taken more seriously at the conference and more generally. We took photos and posted them on social media. I hadn't laughed so much in ages. I'm wearing the moustache while I write this book. If nothing else, wearing it helps me maintain my sense of humour in the face of the challenges I am writing about. I'll talk more about the benefits of having a sense of humour later in the book too.

What's coming up?

The next chapter unpacks more about what is going on for women at universities and provides some context for the dispiriting figures in this first chapter. We delve into why the odds are against women in universities. To be honest, it's a bit depressing. But I promise that after Chapter Two, I will stop making you feel depressed and instead offer you lots of ideas about what to do about the reality you are facing.

CHAPTER TWO

You're Expected to Be a Good Girl

What you're up against

This chapter is about the sexist expectations of women at work in universities – especially, but not only, women in leadership positions. You may not think of yourself as a leader. You may think it is not your ambition to be a leader and you are only interested in advancing up through the academic scales, or up to a higher-level professional appointment. But to advance through the academic or professional levels, you will need to lead. Evidence of you leading is key to your success in academic environments – whether through unit coordination and course coordination; being a research project leader, team leader or group leader; adopting a supervisor, coordinator or manager role; or taking a role as associate head or head of department, or associate dean or dean of a faculty, a director or another sort of senior leader.

If you want to advance, you must understand some of the real and complex forces working against you as a woman in a university, and of the implicit expectations of you as a woman and as a female leader. Many of these forces and expectations are hidden. You need to understand what others are likely to think and expect of you, how you are seen – especially by men – and what assumptions are being made about you. This is what this chapter is about. If you don't understand these hidden forces and knowingly navigate your way through them, you are less likely to end up in a leadership role in a university or to be successful as a leader. Understanding all of this will help you to manage and navigate the assumptions about and expectations of you.

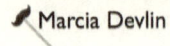
Marcia Devlin

The previous chapter was about the facts related to women in academia and leadership. This chapter looks at why the facts are as they are. Put simply, the facts are as they are because you are expected to be a 'good girl'. In her book, *The Curse of the Good Girl*[5], Psychologist Rachael Simmons explains that a good girl is successful academically and socially, smart and driven and kind. She aims to please others, not have opinions and to follow the rules. She represses and never expresses what she really thinks and tends toward perfectionism. Simmons adds that a good girl 'walked a treacherous line, balancing mixed messages about how far she should go and how strong she should be: she was to be enthusiastic while being quiet; smart with no opinions on things; intelligent but a follower; popular but quiet. She would be something, but not too much'. This chapter explains how women do not advance in universities at the same rate as men partly because we are expected to exist and work in a similar impossible combination of contradictory attributes and behaviours.

Implicit gendered expectations

Walking into my first executive meeting as a new appointee in one workplace, I was quite apprehensive. I had read all the papers carefully, highlighting key points and making notes in the margins. I had spent a lot of time and effort doing this, and I was ready to listen and respond to the contents of the meeting items. My executive colleagues were all men. They were friendly and greeted me informally as I came into the room, or as they came in after me. Then one said, 'Hey, Marcia,' and when I turned to look at him, he gestured with his chin to the cupcakes on plates lining the centre of the table. 'Did you bake these?' And then he laughed – a horse laugh. I'll come back to this story in Chapter Three.

Implicit leadership theory suggests people have implicit expectations and assumptions about leaders' inherent characteristics, traits and qualities. You probably won't be surprised to hear that people have different implicit expectations of male and female leaders, or implicitly expect female leaders to adhere to society's general expectations of women. My own experiences inside Australian universities over three decades has strengthened my belief in this theory.

Colleagues, including superiors, have certain expectations of you because you are a woman. Put simply, you are expected to be a good girl, which is inconsistent with being a good leader. When you understand these expectations, you can choose how much to meet and/or reject them, and learn how to manage them.

'Women's things' – Carpets, curtains and colours

When I was working at one Australian university as an academic, my (male) head of department offered me 'a leadership opportunity'. We were moving offices and the space into which we were moving was a shell in need of refurbishing and decorating. The leadership 'opportunity' was for me to lead this furnishing and decoration work. 'You'd be in charge of everything,' he gushed, breathlessly as he excitedly pitched the idea to me, adding for clarification, 'carpets, curtains, colours... EVERYTHING!'*

I thanked the head for 'thinking of me' (as one learns to do in these preposterous situations) and politely asked for time to consider his offer. He beamed and left my office, clearly delighted with his magnanimous self. I stared out the window, trying to picture the window coverings in my own house. Nothing. I rang my husband. 'Hey, strange question – do we have curtains on our windows at home?' We didn't, apparently. We had blinds.

Anyone who has known me for longer than five minutes knows I have no clue about matters of home or office décor – nor any interest, whatsoever, in learning more. I couldn't care less about carpets, curtains or colours. Every house I have ever owned is painted white – inside and out. The 'artwork' in my home consists of creations by my children when they were very young, placed in cheap picture frames I had either bought at Ikea or found on the side of the road on local council pickup day. While colleagues wouldn't necessarily know this level of detail about my home décor, the time and effort I have ever taken to do anything vaguely resembling decorating my office, other than place a single family photo on my work desk, might give most a little bit of a clue.

The head who offered me this refurbishment 'opportunity' had worked with me for several years, supervised my work and selected me to work closely with him on key department matters. I can guarantee you that we had never discussed décor in any way, shape or form, and that I had never led him to believe I had the slightest interest in the topic.

But I'm a *woman*. The implicit expectation was I would likely be interested in *women's things*. To be clear, I am not disparaging interior design or decorating. One of my closest friends makes her living as an outstanding interior designer and architect, and I admire her and her exceptional talent

---

* I used gendered language in this sentence, usually reserved for women, to make the male head look foolish – e.g., 'gushed, breathlessly'. It worked, didn't it? He looks like an idiot. Which is disappointing because it means that treating a man how a woman is normally treated diminishes him, and that says a lot about how women are valued – even by intelligent, ambitious women like those reading this book.

enormously. I am also slightly envious of her stunning converted-warehouse home. But this line of work is seen as traditionally female, and my male boss's clumsy attempt to help me gain leadership experience was to ask me to lead the decorating and furnishing of the office. He did not ask me to:

- design the strategic plan for the department (heaven knows we needed one);
- create a policy for the fair distribution of departmental work (again, that would have been helpful); or
- represent the department on university committees where I might learn something, meet people and gain experience and exposure.

None of those. Just full rein (or perhaps 'full reign' as queen of the office) over the carpets, curtains and colours.

I tested out the offer with a (female) professor, who I happened to fall into step beside as we left a meeting. She said, 'You're too good for that – you shouldn't be spending your time and energy on those sorts of things.' Based on her validation of the thoughts I already had, I declined the offer to be lead decorator. Suffice to say, this did not go down well with the head. While this wasn't the reason we subsequently fell out, my declining his offer contributed to the breakdown of our relationship.

I'm not making this up. I think he was hurt by my rejection, but I will never be sure because, soon afterwards, we stopped speaking. I do know, though, from comments he made to colleagues passed on to me, that his expectation was I would be pleased with his thoughtfulness and grateful for the leadership 'opportunity' he had presented, which would fit with my ambitions and development needs. I suspect that when I had rejected the offer, he took it as a personal rejection.

One question remains in my mind. Had there been a male at my level, would he have ever been offered this 'leadership opportunity'? I suspect if he were, it would be seen as an attempt to humiliate him by offering him the 'feminine' job of choosing the soft furnishings. A female colleague took up this opportunity I had rejected. In perhaps completely unrelated news, she never advanced beyond senior lecturer and retired at that level.

You may feel you are not subject to sexist implicit expectations at your institution or in your department. You may feel you are not expected to be a good girl. It is true there are workplaces where these expectations of women are absent. There may even be deliberate, proactive methods in play to ensure equality in your workplace. If so, count your blessings – you are in a rare workplace, in my experience of Australian universities. But if you are in the majority of workplaces, you will need to look out for these good girl expectations. They may be obvious, as in my example above, or more hidden and harder to see. Watch carefully in your institution for the next short while and see if you are right.

And by the way, there is nothing wrong with baking cupcakes or refurbishing an office if there is value in them for you. However, there are downsides to your advancement of you always being implicitly expected to be interested in cupcakes, carpets, curtains and colours and to undertake this sort of work. I talk more about these in Chapter Four.

Unconscious gender bias

Unconsciously, we all tend to like and prefer people who look and think like us, and who come from similar backgrounds. If you stop for a moment and think about the people in your life with whom you have chosen to have close relationships, they will inevitably be 'people like me'. This makes sense – of course we want to spend time with people we feel comfortable with. Despite policies about gender-balanced recruitment and promotion panels – and at least partially because they hold most of the leadership positions – men have a disproportionate influence on recruitment and promotion decisions. We have all seen and can recite examples of the 'halo effect', in universities, where a senior man appoints someone like him, apparently regardless of his appointee's competence or fit for the role.

Unconscious gender bias works against women in universities in subtle ways. Women are not imagined in the top jobs. A couple of years ago, I gave an invited guest lecture and workshop on leadership to a group of high-achieving undergraduate students at an exclusive Australian university. They had applied for, and been selected into, a highly competitive and prestigious extracurricular leadership development program. A bright, engaged, intelligent audience. I told them we had limited time for our icebreaker and we had to work quickly. I suggested they not think too deeply about my requests and just respond as quickly as possible.

I then told the students a made-up, detailed story about a sick cat. I asked them to do the following tasks:
- draw and name the cat;
- draw and name the owner of the cat;
- draw and name the vet that the cat owner had taken the sick cat to see; and
- draw and name the CEO of the multinational company at which the vet worked.

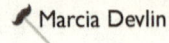
Marcia Devlin

Seventy-five percent of these young, enlightened, future leaders drew a male as the CEO, despite half the group being female. None of those who had drawn the CEO as a man could clearly articulate why they had done so. Several were upset with themselves. I explained that bias happens automatically, without us knowing, through quick assessments and judgements – influenced by our background, environment and personal experiences. We all have biases or ingrained prejudices, whether we know of or admit to them or not. They serve useful biological purposes but are not so useful in the workplace, especially if you're a woman.

> *Most of the people making decisions about your career progression will never undertake the work necessary to uncover and redress their unconscious bias.*

I thought I did not have gender bias (except when I am positively disposed toward females, as I often deliberately am to make my contribution to redressing the imbalance). But I took the gender Implicit Association Test[6] and discovered I was wrong. My results were confronting. Evidently, I had biases and I was not aware of them. Have a go at the test and be prepared to be confronted by your own biases – and the flat feeling that follows when you realise that if you, a woman who has chosen to give up precious free time to read this book, are biased, then what hope do we have? Then please read the rest of the book before you give up the will to go on.

Of course, most of the people making decisions about your career progression will be men and will never take this test – never mind undertake the significant work necessary to uncover and redress their unconscious bias. This is a big problem for women in universities. Facebook Chief Operating Officer Sheryl Sandberg's bestselling book, *Lean In*[7], refers to 'benevolent sexists' – men who hold positive but outdated views about women – and 'nice-guy misogynists' who might believe women are superior in areas like moral reasoning, for example, making them – you guessed it – better equipped to stay home and raise children, and less equipped for the world of work. These terms and notions disturb me, and I can't help wondering sometimes, as I look around a university meeting, with executive and council tables filled with a majority of men, 'How many benevolent nice guys are here today?'

Implicit expectations and unconscious bias combine in challenging ways for women in universities who wish to advance. If you are thinking about ways to advance yourself and articulating this ambition, you are not meeting the gendered expectations to be nice and nurturing *of others*. I was told that a member of the selection panel that had appointed me to a senior position had confided in senior colleagues just after my appointment that I had been selected over other applicants because I 'wasn't too ambitious'. Apparently, a previous female incumbent in the role had been afflicted with too much of this slightly grubby focus on her own career, and this did not go well for her. The sexist male line manager, to whom the role was deputy, evidently needed someone who was more like a 'work wife', happy to be in the background and obviously focused on *his* success, and not her own. Someone who would be a really good girl.

I was told this after a couple of years in the job. I had three thoughts. First, a person who was sharing reflections from a confidential recruitment process should not be on senior appointment or any other selection panels*. Second, at the time I was appointed, I was one of the most ambitious people I knew, so I wondered how I had possibly given the selection panel the false impression that they had formed about me. Perhaps I somehow inadvertently projected the good girl persona they were looking for. Third, these misguided expectations of me, and the significant limitations I had in the role as a result, were probably at the heart of why I really hated the job and ended up deciding to leave before my contract ended.

I don't want to pretend this is an easy matter to address. But awareness of unconscious bias is growing, and I know that a small number of Australian university executive teams have undertaken training in this area. Having more women at the decision-making tables is also likely to help this situation, particularly if they are willing to point out, and, when necessary, call out, gender bias and sexist thinking.

Invisibility

Many women experience implicit expectations and gender bias via invisibility. Invisibility happens in a number of different ways, including being overlooked, being ignored, being interrupted and spoken over and having your ideas repeated and appropriated by others. I have experienced invisibility myself in all these ways, and seen and heard of scores of women having the same experiences.

---

* Unfortunately, she is still on such panels and recently helped a university to replace an outgoing male vice-chancellor with – you guessed it – another male vice-chancellor. Yes, it's a she.

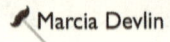
Marcia Devlin

When an internal acting position at a higher level became available at a university I worked at, I was surprised to learn that two male colleagues at the same level as me had been approached about acting in the higher-level role, while I had not.

When I later asked a university council member why this had occurred, he told me, 'You just weren't on our radar'. This was despite my:

- having attended every council meeting for several years;
- leading large and critical strategic projects and, as part of that leadership, presenting regularly to council on the positive progress and impact of those projects;
- having strong working relationships and regular interactions with many council members; and
- being a confident, assured executive who spoke up frequently.

Anyone who has met me will tell you I am far from being a quiet wallflower. I think I was on the council's radar and technically visible, but not for acting promotion – for which they assumed only men had the potential. To his credit, the council member also reflected on our conversation and later followed up with me to tell me, 'You are now on my radar.' He also agreed to be a referee for me in future. But not every woman has the good fortune to have a single interaction with a man who then reflects and changes his awareness and actions.

Every woman who has been in a university meeting has had repetition happen to her or seen it happen to others.

As a woman, you will almost certainly be overlooked for leadership positions, and you may not even know the opportunity existed. You won't be on the decision-makers' radar, even if you think you are or should be. I'll talk more about the word 'should' in Chapter Three and later again.

Another way that women often experience invisibility in meetings is through being completely ignored. The chair will appear to look straight through a woman in front of him who has indicated she'd like to speak. Instead, the chair asks the man next to the woman for his comments. Most women in academia and university management and leadership have experienced this form of invisibility.

Associate Professor Jeannie Rea, former president of the National Tertiary Education Union from 2010 to 2018, has a concept and term for this experience. She says women unwittingly don *an invisibility cloak* in university meetings. Jeannie is a nationally well-known, highly experienced leader with a fierce intellect, well-evidenced views, a strong voice, a deep knowledge of university matters, and yet she told me in 2020 that she frequently feels invisible in meetings. The views of women like Jeannie are often not sought nor heard. Jeannie has also spoken to me about how when a man and a woman collaborate on a project, the man is almost always the one who is asked to report to senior management on that project. Women are literally invisible to the senior decision-makers and the people who might offer opportunities for advancement.

Jeannie and I have also discussed the common experience of invisibility for women through being interrupted and/or spoken over by someone else – usually, but not always, by a man (also known as 'manterruption'). Hands up if you're a woman and you've *never* been interrupted or spoken over in a meeting in a university or have *never* seen another woman interrupted or spoken over by a man. (I don't see any hands.) I offer advice about how to handle being manterrupted in Chapter Three.

Another behaviour that makes women feel they are invisible is repetition. Every single woman who has been in a university meeting has had repetition happen to her or seen it happen to others. Repetition is the experience of a woman saying something in a meeting, being ignored or treated as if she hasn't spoken, and then a man *makes exactly the same point* a few minutes later and is heard. Worse still, the man is sometimes congratulated, even celebrated (and perhaps, on occasion, someone has offered to host a party for him) – such is the recognition of his brilliance as exhibited in the point he just made. You know, *after a woman had already made it, just before he did.* As a woman in academia, it is likely that your ideas will be appropriated this way (or 'bro-propriated' as one of my enlightened male executive colleagues likes to call it – the 'bro' being slang talk for 'brother').

If you think invisibility isn't happening in your part of the academic or professional world, you could have a great and proactive boss, your area is an exception, and every meeting you attend is chaired by a progressive person who ensures equal floor time to everyone, regardless of gender. If this is the case, this is excellent news. Enjoy it and long may it last. But consider the last half-dozen leadership opportunities you were aware of in your institution, and count how many went to women and how many to men. I'd also recommend observing meetings carefully for the next short while. You may start to notice the evidence of women being invisible; that is, overlooked, ignored, manterrupted and/or having their ideas bro-propriated. I have suggestions about how to manage all of this for yourself and for other women later in the book.

Marcia Devlin

The challenge for women of being successful and liked at the same time

You may have heard of the Heidi/Howard experiment[8], which clearly illustrates the dilemmas for women at work. Heidi Roizen was a successful Silicon Valley venture capitalist. Her case study of success was presented to half a business school class with Heidi's name on it. The other half of the class got the same case study, with her name changed to 'Howard'.

The students in the experiment rated Heidi and 'Howard' as equally competent, but they *liked Howard* and *did not like Heidi*. In fact, students felt Heidi was *significantly less likeable*; they perceived her as *more selfish* than Howard and they felt she was *less worthy of being employed* than Howard. These differences in perceptions by students were solely due to them believing that they were considering a woman or a man – the case study was identical in every respect except the subject's name.

While the results of this study are disappointing, they are not surprising to many women. So often in the workplace, we see this sexism and gender discrimination play out. When women dare to exhibit so-called male traits – decisive action, showing authority, being competent – we often dislike them. At the same time, we tend to see men who exhibit those same traits as strong, masculine and competent. When women lead with a confident, direct style, they are often considered to have a 'style issue' – which I talk about more below. Conversely, when men lead confidently and directly, they are simply seen as strong leaders.

The Heidi/Howard experiment, and others like it since, show the mismatch between the qualities traditionally associated with being a woman (e.g., being nice, nurturing and caring) and those traditionally associated with being a leader (e.g., being assertive and dominant). One common implicit expectation of female leaders is that they should be nice and nurturing. There is, of course, nothing wrong with being either nice or nurturing – both are admirable human qualities and, to some extent, the continuity of the human race relies on the existence of both qualities among the population. The existence of these attributes also makes the world a more pleasant place for everyone to live in.

But there are generally stronger expectations of nice, nurturing and/or caring behaviour from a female leader and weaker expectations of the same from a male leader. I have lost count of the number of conversations I have had with colleagues about male leaders with 'low EQ' (low emotional intelligence) and poor ability to support others (but, say, an excellent research record) who are chosen as leaders and then heavily supported by women who do the necessary and critical nurturing and caring leadership work for them. I call this institutional housework, and we'll talk more about this in later chapters.

In her book, Sandberg argues that a central expectation of women is that they should be nurturing and nice above all else. However, she argues that if a woman is perceived as really nice, she may be perceived as more nice than competent. But if she does anything that suggests she may not be 'nice' first and foremost, she will not be liked. Our innate desire to be liked is not only so we feel good – being liked is necessary for professional success. Female leaders, Sandberg argues, find it harder to be successful *and* liked, compared to male leaders. My observations over three decades are that women in universities have to work harder to be seen as well-intentioned, likeable leaders. They need to spend more time and effort than men do in building relationships, being inclusive, encouraging dialogue and demonstrating that they have the wellbeing of others and the greater good of the university as priorities.

Implicit leadership theory suggests that people evaluate a leader's effectiveness in terms of how well that leader fits *preconceived* beliefs about the features and behaviours of effective leaders, which are, of course, different for men and women. When it comes to performance reviews and line manager views, I've yet to see a trend emerging of male leaders being told they are doing fine but that they need to 'focus on softening your style a little'. But women leaders are often given such feedback. Women also miss out on opportunities if they are perceived as 'selfish' – like poor old Heidi (and not good old Howard, who was apparently a really top bloke, even though he accepted credit for a woman's work and didn't even exist).

When you understand the odds and the reasons for the odds, you will be in a better position to navigate the sexism and beat those odds.

In their book on women and leadership[9], where they interview eight female world leaders and draw lessons from these most senior women, former Australian Prime Minister Julia Gillard and her co-author Ngozi Okonjo-Iweala, the former finance minister for Nigeria, dedicate a whole chapter to 'the style conundrum'. They posit that, for political leaders, comparable behaviours elicit different reactions depending on whether the leader is male or female.

Closer to home for most readers of this current book, Gillard and Okonjo-Iweala also reference a 2015 American study conducted at North Carolina State University[10]. In this study, online teachers (who could not be seen or heard by students) both taught a class as themselves and a second class while pretending to be the opposite gender to their own. Guess what? When the performance of the male teacher pretending to be a woman was evaluated by students, he got poorer evaluations than when the students knew he was a man. The female scored higher when the students thought she was a man than when she revealed she was a woman. These sorts of results are not unique to this study. In another study from the University of Florida[11], a class thought they had two teaching assistants – one male and one female. Guess what? The students scored the male higher and the female got *five times* as many negative reviews. But the male and the female were actually the same person.

All of this – and possibly especially these last two examples – may leave you feeling deflated or even defeated. If so, this is understandable. I did warn you that Chapter Two would be depressing. But when you understand the odds and the reasons for the odds, you will be in a better position to navigate the sexism and beat those odds. I also told you that after Chapter Two I will stop making you feel depressed and instead offer you lots of ideas about what to do about the reality you are facing – so you can look forward to that. For now, though, there's a bit more depressing news to go before we get to the good bit. Hang in there.

Balancing gravitas and humility

Women are constantly performing balancing acts to try to meet the implicit and unconscious gendered expectations of them in universities. One lesson you may need to learn is the need to balance gravitas and humility.

A few years ago, I applied and was interviewed for a deputy vice-chancellor position at a university. I was already a DVC at another university but, for family reasons, I wanted to move. My application was unsuccessful. The feedback on my application and interview included a view by members of the recruitment panel that I had 'lacked gravitas' in the interview. I reflected critically on my interview performance, consulted a mentor and some trusted colleagues and worked on my gravitas.

I was shortlisted for another university DVC role soon after. This time, I tried to behave in the way that my search engine had advised are synonyms for gravitas: with status, eminence, greatness, importance, majesty, loftiness, grandeur and lordliness. I felt uncomfortable as behaving even a tiny bit this way went against the grain for me. But I really wanted this job, so I tried my best to have a small bit of the necessary gravitas while remaining true to myself. My application was unsuccessful. This time I was told that members of the recruitment panel felt I had 'lacked humility'.

Humility is an expected attribute of women. To succeed as a woman in academia, you will probably have to outperform others, but definitely not talk about it too much. Take Kamala Harris – the American vice-president. An article by Megan Garber in *The Atlantic*[12] in November 2020 discusses Harris' ambition and her 'conditioned humility'. Garber suggests, '...the reality is the idea that women who achieve things *aren't supposed to say so* [emphasis added] ... It has to do with the fact that, regardless of our own gender, we still tend to view women as self-sacrificial and self-effacing, first and foremost – mothers, basically, whether they have children or not'.

Perhaps, in my second interview, I didn't get the balance between gravitas and humility right. Perhaps, like a (male) friend of mine recently suggested, gravitas is an inherently sexist notion and expectation of leadership that has come from the fact that the course of human history has mostly involved men in leadership roles. Perhaps, like Heidi, I just wasn't liked because I was female. Of course, it may have been that I simply wasn't the best candidate for either job. Both of the jobs went to blokes, by the way. At the time of writing, one is acting vice-chancellor at the same university and the other has advanced to vice-chancellor at a different university. Leadership opportunities lead to advancement, and that's why you need to successfully navigate sexism to get the opportunities you deserve, but which may be disproportionately going to the males.

Just after those two interviews, as I nursed my hurt and disappointment, I read that Adam Grant and Sheryl Sandberg found a meta-analysis of 95 studies showed that, although men are more confident about their leadership ability, women are rated more competent than men in leadership skills by those they work with[13].

But I continue to wonder how women can demonstrate their competence, as well as the expected leadership qualities of assertiveness and dominance, while appearing nice, nurturing and caring, all the while having the requisite amounts and balance of gravitas and humility, especially as we know all the while what happened to poor Heidi?

Marcia Devlin

What happens if you are a woman and perceived as not nice?

Having a woman in leadership can be threatening and difficult for some people, both male and female, in universities. This is especially true if a woman rejects the implicit expectations of her to be nice, nurturing and 'mothering' in her leadership style and approach to the leadership role. When this 'lack' of 'softness' is accompanied by an approach that focuses on outcomes and deliverables and/or includes candour about the performance of direct reports that may be below par, the result can be a person feeling threatened by a(n assertive) woman.

One of the potential consequences of not being liked or being perceived as 'not nice', as a woman, is that colleagues may undermine you as a way to slow you down/trip you up/put you back in your box. Many women I know who work in academia have experienced undermining. Often, it is covert and you feel like you know it's happening but can't always see or point to hard evidence of it. Less commonly, it is overt and then you know for sure.

I have experienced a lot of undermining during my academic career. Even being in a senior role does not protect you as undermining can be achieved effectively through subtle means. These include, for example:

- an 'innocently overlooked' email that you have sent and to which you receive no response;
- a 'misunderstanding' about what a request was seeking;
- a colleague taking too long to respond to a request for information, which results in a deadline being missed;
- a perceived 'lack of clarity' about some matter that leads to delay, misinformation, confusion or the claimed need to revisit your decision; and
- 'accidentally' excluding you from a meeting, conversation and/or emails.

Both men and women in universities experience undermining, but it is more common for women, and even more common for women who are not playing by the gender rules set for them.

Another potential consequence of not meeting gendered expectations that many women experience is gossiping/bad mouthing and rumour spreading. Women are far more often victims than men. Malicious gossip can be about your character, 'style', management of emotions, personal life or any other aspect of your personhood. This has happened to me many times. In one example, a colleague told me she had been told by a very senior person in the university with a lot of influence that 'everyone knew' that I was 'not a team player'. I found this galling, given the value I place on teamwork and the time and effort I always put into being part of the teams in which I work. But, of course, the nasty gossiper knew this – she targeted the unfounded gossip so it would be most hurtful and harmful to me.

Even if the gossip is completely untrue (as it often is), throwing mud like this is effective in creating wariness and even dislike or distrust of a woman. This, in turn, can successfully undermine your efforts to build relationships, camaraderie, teams and harmonious workplaces. It can also harm your reputation and undermine your ambitions and goals. In some cases, it can create even greater damage and negatively affect your mental health.

> *Gender judo is training yourself to behave in a 'warm and nurturing' way with just a sprinkling of Mother Superior.*

Sexism isn't just a problem in universities. All workplaces are sexist – it's just a matter of degree. If you don't agree, show me a workplace where men and women are exactly even in terms of opportunity, leadership, pay and all the other measures. If you can find this workplace, it is unique or rare. In her essay, 'Men at Work: Australia's Parenthood Trap'[14], Annabel Crabb points out that we have the term 'working mum' for a mother who works but that 'working dad' isn't a thing.

Joan Williams, a law professor and co-author of *What Works for Women at Work*[15], interviewed hundreds of women and offers a solution to the dilemmas and contradictions and impossible situations I outline above – 'gender judo'. Gender judo is training yourself to behave in a 'warm and nurturing' way with just a sprinkling of Mother Superior, so you can get the respect you need for a cohesive workplace. Referring to this concept, writer Natalie Reilly suggests that being 'likeable' for women at work seems to equate with being obsequious and conformist[16].

Getting your style 'right'

But wait, there's more. Most university senior women I know have had 'the style' conversation at least once in their career. The style conversation goes something like this. The line manager of the female staff member asks for a meeting, or raises the matter during a performance review meeting. There has been 'feedback' about the woman in question, and it's not positive, unfortunately. There is apparently a concern about her 'style', which is creating a little bit of angst. You see, her style is just a little bit – how shall I put this – brusque, abrupt at times, tending toward blunt, sometimes terse, has an element of briskness about it, and can be a little bit sharp. She has been known to be short, on occasion. She cut someone off when he was speaking last month (or was it last year? The details and examples are sometimes a bit vague and hard to recall). If you haven't had this conversation yet and you are a woman with a leadership role or ambition, it's more than likely coming. I'll talk about how to handle this conversation in the next chapter.

Style is something that male leaders in universities generally need to give little thought to. None of the senior men I have asked about the style conversation have understood what I was talking about. Men generally put on clothes, go to work, get promoted and get put in charge. Not so for the women, unfortunately. I'll talk more about style and provide some advice later in the book.

Conclusion

Let's recap. As a woman in a university:
- you are implicitly expected to enjoy baking, home decorating and 'womanly things', which aren't aligned with traditional notions of leadership;
- you will be the subject of unconscious discriminatory bias because you are female;
- you will be invisible in a number of ways, including to the decision-makers searching for appropriate colleagues to whom they can offer leadership opportunities;
- your views and voice will not be sought or heard;
- you will be continually manterrupted and spoken over;
- your good ideas will be appropriated and claimed by others;
- you will need to be, above all else, nice and nurturing – as all good women should be;
- you must carefully balance gravitas and humility, if you want to be a leader;
- you will need to work extremely hard, and potentially much harder than most men, but not talk about it, to ensure you are liked and not considered selfish or self-serving;
- you are likely to be undermined and may be gossiped about;

- you need to engage in gender judo to be likeable; and
- you must have the 'right' style for a woman.

Got it?

You might think things can't be as bad as I have outlined in this chapter. You might think I am being overly negative or that all of this doesn't apply to you. You are not alone. When I was testing out some of the ideas I wanted to put in this book, I asked a female associate professor colleague this question: 'Do you think you have ever been discriminated against on the basis of your gender?' She replied immediately, 'No, I don't think so.' I waited as she stared into the middle distance, deep in thought. 'Other than having done a LOT of administration, with no time release and no research funding, and more and more teaching when I returned from mat. leave,' she said. I waited. 'I mean, I've seen a LOT of men promoted before me – but they all had a wife at home looking after the kids. I was the wife at home looking after the kids,' she said. I waited. 'I mean, I've seen things that are a bit blokey. Like men getting more opportunities than women – like on research grants with other men, for example.' So, no gender discrimination for my colleague then?

You might wonder why some women make it at all in universities, if things are as dire as I have outlined in this chapter. Things are as they are. Not all of this will apply to every woman, and some women do make it, despite all of this. I made it – to professor and then later to director, executive director, deputy vice-chancellor, senior vice-president and senior deputy vice-chancellor. I am a globally recognised scholar in my field with a bestowed lifelong membership to my discipline research society. Every single thing I have talked about in this chapter has happened to me and/or I have observed them happening to other women, more than once.

For a long time, I thought there was something wrong with me. But now I know better. Every senior woman working in an Australian university has had similar experiences. Ask any of them. Most of us navigated it alone, or mostly alone. I don't want you to have to do this alone, so this book is for you. When the things I have described in this chapter and the previous chapter, or other horrible things, happen to you, I want you to know it's not you – it's almost certainly, at least partly, the sexism that exists in Australian universities.

You don't have to take it. The rest of the book is about how to navigate the sexism you have probably experienced and will probably continue to experience. As you read my book, consider the advice in it carefully and set to work applying whichever of the suggestions offered appeals to you, in your particular circumstances and at your particular stage of career.

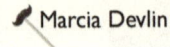
Marcia Devlin

Buy a copy for each of your female colleagues and then go online and wax lyrical about how this book changed your life so that lots of other people buy it too. Then I can become rich and famous, buy some black skivvies and a new false moustache, go on book tours looking like a male author and make a fortune from book sales so that I never have to go to another university meeting and be manterrupted or have my ideas bro-propriated again. In addition to helping me to sell lots of books, the more women who know about what is happening to them, the more we can individually and collectively push back, and change things for ourselves and for the women coming up behind us.

What's coming up?

The next chapter offers the first piece of advice for women aspiring to advance in universities: *Get an attitude*.

CHAPTER THREE

Get an Attitude

What are you going to do about it?

In the previous two chapters we discussed your odds of succeeding as a woman in higher education. As I explained, they aren't great. I also explained the sexist (and other) forces working against you and against your progress. Those forces are strong. The question now is, what are you going to do about it?

When I have asked some women this question, I often get a response about how 'the system' should change, the structural barriers should be removed, HR should start a mentoring program, senior leaders should do something, or the university should do something. I certainly agree with all of these (and some other) 'shoulds'. The problem is that, to date, these things that 'should' happen haven't happened, or at least not consistently. Or they haven't happened in ways that lead to consistently better outcomes for women – at least not in the almost 30 years that I've worked in the university sector. While these things 'should' happen, some of them are happening and maybe they will start to balance the odds in time. But, in the meantime, you will also need to decide what you are going to do.

Getting an attitude

The structural and systemic barriers to women succeeding in universities at the same rate as men are not within your control. You need to focus on what is within your sphere of control – or at least your sphere of influence. To do this effectively, you need to get an attitude.

More specifically, you must carefully choose the attitude or attitudes that you will bring to your navigation of the poor odds and the sexism you will face. These attitudes will need to fit with your personal circumstances and goals. The attitudes you choose will either help or hinder you in managing your individual circumstances and meeting your personal objectives. We'll talk more about your specific personal goals in Chapter Four.

There are many options for attitudes that you can adopt. These include attitudes of: helplessness, knowing, confidence, anger, acceptance, calm, determination, humour and working smarter, not harder. I'll discuss each of these briefly below. Whichever attitude you choose at a particular time or in a particular situation, choose one that suits you as a unique individual – you first need to be true to yourself.

> *You must carefully choose the attitude or attitudes that you will bring to your navigation of the poor odds and the sexism you will face.*

Being yourself

Whatever attitudes you choose to adopt to navigate sexism, make sure they fit with your values and principles and with your personality. Be yourself. However, being a 'good girl' (which many of us are, at least most of the time) has not helped us collectively to advance in universities at the same rate as men, so we must keep that in mind. We all have versions of ourselves and of 'the real me'. The version of you that presents when teaching students is different to the version of you that we might meet on a social night out with your closest friends. Both are authentic, genuine and 'you'. It's useful to think about being yourself – but a particular version of yourself – depending on the circumstances and needs of the situation.

Some of the most commonly adopted attitudes are described below. Assess each and how closely it fits with you 'being yourself'. There are examples later in the chapter about how to apply attitudes. This list is not exhaustive, and you may have different attitudes you wish to adopt.

A helpless attitude

'Learned helplessness' is a well-known psychological phenomenon. If you ever took first-year psychology, you might remember that this arose from research by Martin Seligman[17] with animals who were restrained and then administered electric shocks. At first, the animals jump around, trying to avoid the shock, which is impossible to avoid because of the restraints. After some time, they give up trying to avoid the shock and instead passively accept it each time – they have learned to be helpless. When the animals are moved to another situation where they can easily avoid shocks by moving, they don't bother and continue to passively accept the shocks.

In humans, learned helplessness stems from a person having an unpleasant experience repeatedly. They come to believe that they are helpless to prevent or control unpleasant experiences, no matter what they do – even when this is not the case. They learn to feel helpless, regardless of their situation.

Gender discrimination and sexism affect us in similar ways to receiving shocks, in that the more often you experience it and see it happening around you, the more you are prone to learned helplessness in the face of it. You can choose to adopt this attitude, but if you do then I would recommend you stop reading here – there's no point in continuing with this book. Hopefully, you will not stop here and will instead actively avoid an attitude of learned helplessness as feeling and being helpless will not help you in your navigation.

A knowing attitude

Your armoury of attitudes to navigate the sexism you are facing, and will continue to face, might include a knowing attitude. This means you adopt an attitude based on knowing about the data, knowing about the rate of change, knowing about the sexism that permeates Australian universities and knowing that the odds are against you. That's it. It is helpful (if also sometimes annoying) to remind yourself of what you know from the evidence. If you're female, you're less likely to make it to the top of academia – know that. This attitude is helpful in motivating me to continue doing all I can to eradicate sexism and gender discrimination in universities.

A confident attitude

A confident attitude is helpful with most endeavours. There's no point starting off by telling yourself, 'This will never work' or, 'This will be a waste of time.' If you are thinking thoughts like that, try to override them with replacement thoughts like, 'I'm going to give this a red-hot go' and, 'This will be interesting, maybe even fun.' You often get what you expect, and if you expect to get nowhere, it's more likely than not that nowhere is exactly where you will end up. Conversely, if you expect to get somewhere, you're also more likely to achieve that. It can't hurt to be confident in your attitude.

Marcia Devlin

An angry attitude

Being angry about sexism and gender discrimination is natural and common. Most women I've spoken to about this demonstrate a level of anger about the situation. Sometimes, the more they find out, the angrier they become. Anger can be great as it alerts us to the fact that something is wrong. It helps us understand there is a problem to be worked through and resolved. Anger can also work as a useful source of motivation. I am writing this book, determined to finish it, and I will ensure it is published. My drive for all of this comes at least partly from the anger I feel about the unfairness of the sexism suffered currently by women in Australian universities and that I have suffered throughout my university career.

However, be careful about slipping from a healthy level of motivating anger to a 'smash the patriarchy' level of anger in your attitude. The latter can be dangerous at best and counterproductive at worst. As I explained in Chapter One, the people making the important decisions in universities are mostly men. Whether you like it or not, men will play a big part in whether you get promoted or offered leadership opportunities. Therefore, men will play a key part in your advancement in academia. Being obviously angry with them will not help them see the value of having you and other women as equals.

The enlightened men in universities — and there are a growing number of them — recognise and promote (literally and figuratively) the value-add of having women in senior roles and at decision-making tables. These men understand the benefits of the diversity of perspective and opinion that women bring to teams, departments and institutions. But not all men in universities are enlightened. We have all worked with men who happily and steadfastly cling to the old ways that made them successful, and thus ensure that they surround themselves with people like them and people who agree with them. While it's understandable to feel like you'd like to smash the patriarchy in universities, harbouring, showing or acting on such feelings is unproductive and unhelpful to your navigation at this stage of human evolution. Dialling your feelings back to a level of anger that can be harnessed and used for good is advisable.

A word of caution: an angry attitude in a woman is not considered 'ladylike' and, as we learned in Chapter Two, there are gendered expectations of you. You need to be aware that if you show you are angry, you are likely to be perceived as 'too emotional' (somewhat expected for a woman but not good) or 'aggressive' (really not good). If you are seen as angry, your views are less likely to be listened to than if you appear calm and rational —

attributes that are valued regardless of gender. Better to keep those angry cards close. Be pleasant and apparently emotionally neutral on the surface, but use the anger you feel to motivate you internally to do whatever you think will best help your situation at the time. All of that said, I recommend adopting anger as an attitude.

An accepting attitude

In contrast to the helpless attitude mentioned above, it can be useful for you to adopt an accepting attitude. You can, for example, note the evidence presented in Chapters One and Two, quietly accept that the odds are stacked against you and leave things at that. You can accept that, despite your current or future needs – for growth, new challenges, opportunities, higher-level roles, more satisfaction at work and higher pay – your gender means you're not likely to get these things, and you can just accept that. This sort of acceptance is not accompanied by feelings of helplessness, it is simply a quiet acquiescence to the way things are – at least for now.

Sometimes, women decide that they want advancement, but not now or not just yet. I have mentored many women with small children who have come to the realisation that, at certain stages of their children's lives, they want to spend less time at work and more time with their children. Having considered everything relevant carefully – including their children and family's needs, their partner's commitments, their level of support from others, the resources available to them and other factors – they determine that, for now, they will accept the situation and that their careers will not advance for a time. I completely understand and support an accepting attitude and these sorts of decisions. They are highly personal and individual.

At one time, I knowingly adopted an accepting attitude myself. I was a lecturer (at Level B) for over 12 years while I started my family and raised children as the primary caregiver. As a migrant, with no family support in the state in which my partner and I lived, I was the primary caregiver to two children – one of whom was very sick, and in and out of hospital for years. I worked part-time, undertook study and professional registration requirements, kept writing and publishing as far as was humanly possible, and held onto my career by the skin of my teeth.

While I don't recommend that you adopt a long-term accepting attitude to successfully navigate the sexism you will continue to face, it is there for you to choose if your circumstances dictate that it is the best option for you at a particular time.

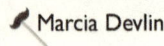
Marcia Devlin

A calm attitude

A calm attitude is different from an attitude of acceptance. Calmness is helpful for a number of reasons. Being calm is an antidote to anxiety and to worry, neither of which are particularly helpful in methodically assessing and then addressing a large problem or challenge. Sexism is a complex, nuanced and difficult problem. Becoming agitated about it is not going to help – not in the long run. Remaining calm helps you to think more clearly and this, in turn, helps you to make better decisions.

While not a naturally calm person myself, I work hard on adopting an attitude of calm or, at the very least, an outer appearance of calm. I actively work on being calm, primarily through irregular but frequent meditation. Being calm means it is less likely that the gendered criticism of being 'too emotional' often levelled at women will be used with you. This takes one weapon out of the armoury used against women. I highly recommend this option.

A determined attitude

Given the odds of your success in academia, if you want to overcome them then you will need a lot of determination. This means setting your sights on a set of goals or objectives, committing to these and resolving not to deviate from their pursuit. Determination is often discussed alongside resilience. Resilience supports determination and is covered in Chapter Six. For now, adopting an attitude of being determined to beat the odds will serve you well. How that determination translates into action will depend on the situation and a range of related factors, but having and showing resolve will be helpful to you. I recommend adopting an attitude of determination.

A humorous attitude

While some of what happens to women in academia is dispiriting, demotivating, annoying or downright infuriating, I have found some situations can have a funny side. I have a natural tendency toward seeing the humorous side of situations, and I often adopt this in my attitude to dealing with sexist and other difficult experiences.

In an earlier chapter, I told the story of the male head of department who thought he was helping me by offering me the lead in a redecoration project ('Carpets, curtains and colours'). What I didn't say was that, following my rejection of his offer, he led a bullying campaign in turning others against me, which led to my mental health being negatively affected. While I was dealing with his abhorrent behaviour, I adopted an alternative name for him to use with some women in the department while laughing about him behind his back. His new name was close to his real name, but was also the name of a well-known, ditzy female reality TV star at the time. Adopting this name for him and laughing at him helped me get through one of the worst experiences of my career.

Psychologists call this behaviour 'cognitively restructuring'. This means thinking about your situation in ways that make you feel better. If this man has the status of an airhead and D-grade celebrity in my mind, it becomes easier to survive and recover from his terrible treatment of me. I even got to the point of waving to him in a (fake) friendly way across a room at a work function once. I swear I saw his knees buckle when I did that. I did report his appalling behaviour to his seniors at the university while it was happening. They did nothing, and he was subsequently promoted several times. But constructing him in my mind as a laughable, pathetic character helped me both to cope and to recover and move on. It can be empowering – not to mention great fun – to adopt a humorous attitude and have a laugh about your challenges and the people who create them for you.

Humour needs to be used and adopted judiciously. That said, I recommend adopting humour as an attitude if it comes naturally to you and feels comfortable.

A 'work smarter, not harder' attitude

A 'work smarter, not harder' attitude can be quite useful when navigating sexism. It's likely to work for you for a few reasons. First, you are already smart. You've overcome the sexist barriers that have been there all your life, and you have made it as far as you have so far. Well done! That's not an easy thing to do and is not possible without a high level of intelligence. Second, you've recently gotten even smarter. You bought this book and have read this far – you're wiser as a result. Even if nothing I've said so far is completely new information, seeing it all laid out has consolidated and validated some hunches you've had for a while. Third, we all understand the benefits of strategically and thoughtfully allocating our limited resources to selected priorities rather than trying to do everything equally well.

The 'work smarter, not harder' attitude is where you acknowledge the realities and sources of power in universities, and then think and act in the best interests of your advancement at all times. I'm not very good at adopting this attitude myself, but I understand that it's a good one and I keep trying. I recommend that you also attempt to adopt this attitude.

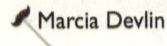
Marcia Devlin

Your attitudes at work

Above, we have considered the attitudes of helplessness, knowing, confidence, anger, acceptance, calm, determination, humour and working smarter, not harder. Below, I give some examples of where particular attitudes have been applied to specific work situations. There are countless combinations of attitude and situation interacting with your principles and personality – the examples below are for you to consider and prompt your thinking about which attitudes you might adopt in which situations.

I recommend adopting a calm, determined and working smarter attitude, and specifically being unpredictable, to any woman who is managing undermining colleagues and/or situations.

Handling implicit expectations with attitude

Remember when I told you in Chapter One about my first executive meeting in one workplace? The one where one of my male colleagues gestured to the cupcakes on the executive table and asked me whether I had baked them? Here's how I handled that conversation with attitude. For the purposes of explanation, I'll call my colleague 'Fred'.

The initial attitude I adopted was one of calm. I was shocked by Fred's 'joke', especially because my emotions were already heightened by being in my first executive meeting in a new job. Adopting a calm attitude was helpful to managing those emotions. Next, I turned my body around so I was facing Fred. I did this slowly, for effect, and also to give myself time to collect my thoughts and formulate my response. While I slowly swivelled and settled, I adopted a slightly angry, determined, working smarter attitude. The anger was under the surface, giving me poise. The determination ensured I said something (I'm not one to keep quiet).

I knew I had to be smart – whatever I said would set up my working relationship with this man and, possibly, albeit to a lesser extent, the other men in the room. I smiled pleasantly at Fred. The smile was fake. I'm not sure whether that was obvious or not – it works either way, so that doesn't matter. Fred smiled back. Next, I asked Fred, 'Are you asking me that question because women bake and I'm the only woman here?'

Asking a question about his 'joke' had the effect of dismantling it. Jokes are often not funny after someone deconstructs them or asks why the joke teller thinks they are funny. Fred was no longer smiling and had begun to look uncomfortable. My question laid bare the inherent sexism in the 'joke', which, when it is made explicit, is obviously not acceptable in a university setting. Fred became flustered and blurted, 'It was just a joke!' No-one laughed. I kept eye contact with Fred. The vice-chancellor then entered the room to commence the meeting and the conversation ended.

I had other choices in the moment when Fred asked whether I was the baker of the cupcakes. I could have ignored him, either feigning deafness and pretending I hadn't heard him or simply not responding, despite clearly hearing what he said. I could have laughed at his 'joke', as I have done in other similar awkward situations. I could have given him one of my 'looks' (they can be quite withering, apparently). I could have blushed, lowered my head, teared up, told him angrily not to be ridiculous or left the room. There is no right response. There is no way to tell what will work best in a given situation ahead of time, and you are usually caught off-guard by these sorts of moments. This is one of the reasons I recommend choosing the attitudes you want to use ahead of time and selecting an overall attitude or combination of attitudes to draw on as you navigate your way through sexism. When something unexpected happens, you are then ready, or readier than you would have otherwise been, and can respond appropriately.

The postscript to this story is that Fred realised what he had done had been thoughtless and potentially harmful. After the meeting, he apologised to me and told me he had meant no harm. He told me he had realised what he said was a stupid thing to say, even in jest, and that it wasn't funny. He subsequently became a quiet supporter and occasional confidante, checking in on how I was going from time to time.

Handling undermining with bad girl attitude

One of the best pieces of advice I got as a female leader and when dealing with poorly behaved men reporting to me was from an experienced senior (male) colleague. He was mentoring me secretly because he was a good bloke and he wanted to help. It had to be secret because when I asked my male line manager if we could appoint this person as my mentor, he said no. (As an aside, you might have noticed that after my line manager said 'no', I didn't accept his decision and go back to my office like a good girl. I adopted a determined attitude – some might say contrary attitude – and went ahead and engaged with the mentor anyway, on different terms.)

'The trouble with you, Marcia,' the secret mentor began one day, after I had my usual debrief about the undermining behaviour from male colleagues that I was experiencing, 'is you have high standards, you hold yourself to them, you expect others to be held to them, and you are utterly predictable in all of that.' He said all this like it was a bad thing. He went on to say that 'the boys' – as he referred to my troublesome colleagues – all knew *exactly* what I was going to do next (the right thing), and that they could predict and plan for that 'every single day'. They were, according to my secret mentor, 'playing with me', undermining my authority, doing things 'deliberately to upset' me, 'conspiring with each other to have greater negative effect' and, to top it off, 'really enjoying themselves'.

I felt humiliated, which pretty quickly gave way to fury, and asked what I should do. 'Flip this,' he advised 'and become unpredictable'. He explained that as well as 'throwing the boys off their games', his prediction was they would begin to have more respect for me if I wasn't behaving so well. Looking back, I see that this mentor was telling me to stop being a good girl.

After sleeping on it, the next day I adopted a calm, determined, working smarter attitude and decided to take his advice to become unpredictable. I cancelled all my regular, planned 1:1 meetings with each of 'the boys' for the rest of the year. I wrote a sweet, personalised email to each of them. I told each of them that I had been reflecting on our working relationship and that, following that reflection, I didn't think I was meeting their needs as a leader. I quoted negative feedback they had given to our senior boss, including about my 'style'. I told each of them I had cancelled our planned meetings and, instead, given I had an open-door policy, invited them to pop in or arrange to meet with me whenever they chose to do so. I signed off, noting that I hoped my efforts to make a change would prompt an improved working relationship.

If only because they were all now wary of me and unsure about what I would do next, the poor behaviour and undermining reduced significantly. My relationships with each of them improved slightly – if only on the surface. They all eventually asked to have regular 1:1 meetings reinstated. I should say that my behaviour in cancelling meetings is not role-model behaviour of excellent leadership. But being a good girl and doing the right thing as a leader wasn't working and was facilitating the continued undermining, so it was worth a radical shake up in that circumstance.

I continued to be unpredictable in small ways. I made a point of:
- sometimes not following up on (non-critical) matters for them, as they often did to me;
- 'forgetting' to do things I'd agreed to do, as they often did;
- cancelling an arranged meeting at short notice from time to time, as they had done frequently previously;
- asking one of them, at short notice, to chair a difficult committee meeting. Twice.

In other words, I continued in similar small ways to be a bad girl.

I have shared this technique with a few senior women – in universities and in other industries. All of them have reported back that it has had positive impacts. One reported a joyous feeling of liberation from being 'a good girl'. Another reported satisfaction in disarming 'the opposition', as she described her male colleagues. Several have described a shift in wariness from themselves about their troublesome colleagues to the other way around where the troublesome colleagues became wary. I recommend adopting a calm, determined and working smarter attitude, and specifically being unpredictable, to any woman who is managing undermining colleagues and/or situations.

Handling being manterrupted with attitude

When I first started working at one university where the culture was very masculine and manterrupting women was normal and accepted, I was taken aback. After a while of adopting an attitude of calm confidence, anger and determination immediately after I was manterrupted, I started saying, 'I haven't finished.' If the person who had manterrupted me kept going with their manterruption, I'd repeat, 'I haven't finished.' Apparently, I also had 'a look' that accompanied this exchange, and often 'a tone'. Reportedly, all of this made people scared to manterrupt me or to manterrupt other women when I was present. Eventually, they were scared to manterrupt other women even when I wasn't present. Complaints were made to my boss about my look, my tone and my 'style'. A coach was appointed to assist me with my style. No, I am not making this up. I talk more about style below.

American politician Kamala Harris – the vice-president of America – became my 2020 girl crush. In the vice-presidential debate in early October 2020, her opponent interrupted and spoke over her. She said, politely, 'Mr Vice-President, I'm speaking.' He ignored her and continued with his manterruption. She repeated, a tiny bit more forcefully, 'I'm speaking.' He stopped. The world's media dissected her repeated retort and it was widely reported. She gained new social media followers and became a role-model for women everywhere. Just after the debate, the American President at the time referred to her as a 'monster' and 'unlikeable'.*

---

* I've deliberately not used the name of any of the men in this anecdote. The subject – and therefore, the centre of my story – is the woman, so I've highlighted her and made the men background characters. Basically, I've reversed what usually happens in the majority of films and TV series and in life generally. It feels good, I have to say.

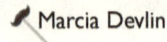 Marcia Devlin

Closer to home in November 2020, an ABC television *4 Corners* program titled, 'Inside the Canberra Bubble'[18], revealed strong evidence of a sexist culture in the federal government. The next day, the male prime minister and a senior female minister faced the press. The female minister was asked about her experience and perception, as a woman, of the culture in government. She began to answer the question the journalist had asked her. The male prime minister manterrupted her and gave his answer to the question before allowing her to speak.

The New York Times contributing columnist and editor Jessica Bennett offers these excellent ideas to countering **manterruptions**[19]:

- Establish a 'no interruptions' rule in meetings. When someone is speaking, they are enabled to finish, without interruption. If you are not the chair with the power to establish such a rule, suggest this to the chair in an offline conversation.
- Practise bystander intervention. You can do this by interrupting him politely and asking him to let the person speaking finish or telling him you want to hear what the woman has to say. If you are nearby and COVID-safe protocols allow, gently nudge or elbow him. Intervene.
- Create a buddy system with a male colleague before the meeting. Ask him to look interested when you speak and to nod when he agrees with you. Ask him to back you up publicly. Ask him to ask manterrupters to 'shhhhhhhhhhhh'.

Bennett suggests that, if all else fails, you can always learn how to talk really, really loud. I'd add that you should do so in a deep voice. While wearing your false moustache.

I have been manterrupted a lot during my nearly 30-year career in higher education in Australia. It has had a cumulative irritating effect on me over that time. But I was surprised that the more senior I became, the more it happened. That seems counter-intuitive, right? I have an emerging theory that it might be because the more senior a woman becomes, the more she is challenging the gender stereotypes, and, therefore, the more threatening she becomes in the minds of people who are not comfortable with women being equal or, heaven forbid, senior to them. I now know that when someone manterrupts me, and especially if he doesn't back down when the fact that he's interrupted me is pointed out, this says a lot about what is going on in his mind – consciously or unconsciously.

Once I was reporting to a man who manterrupted me – every single time – I spoke in our team meetings. He added a gesture of raising his flat palm vertically in the air facing towards me (like a stop sign). It was pretty annoying and dispiriting. I decided to raise the matter with him and did so at the end of a regular 1:1 meeting, in a respectful and polite way, and with a determined, calm attitude. As I explained the issue, saying, 'When I speak in our team meetings, you interrupt me and raise your hand to me—' he manterrupted me, made his usual stop-sign hand gesture toward me, and said, 'No I don't.' We both looked at his hand, suspended in the air between us. 'I think we can both see that you do,' I said quietly. He looked in wonderment at his own hand. To his credit, now aware of his behaviour, he subsequently did try not to manterrupt me and the behaviour did decrease, although it did not stop.

When I am manterrupted now, I say, every time, '[Person's name], I haven't finished.' I repeat it as many times as is necessary until the person speaking stops speaking. I do this with a knowing, confident and calm attitude. Sometimes I smile pleasantly between my protests. Sometimes I'm angry – especially if it's a repeat offender – and that shows a little. I can live with that. I expect to be interrupted and I am ready with the appropriate attitude to address this.

Handling bro-propriation with attitude

Remember when I told you about women feeling invisible because of repetition in meetings? You say something, it is ignored and then one of the 'bros' repeats it a few minutes later and the room erupts into a chorus of 'For he's a jolly good fellow'? Every single woman I have mentored has experienced bro-propriation. Every. Single. One. It's remarkable. And infuriating.

A few years ago, I'd had enough and I adopted an attitude of calm, confident anger and of being smarter (a killer combo, just quietly). I started calling bro-propriation out. I do the following: When a woman's ideas are repeated by a man in a meeting, I say something like, 'Great idea [insert man's name]. I'm not sure if you heard it, but that's exactly what [insert woman's name] said just a moment ago.' Sometimes I get a response like, 'Yeah but I think...' from the man. I politely wait for him to finish before repeating the point that [insert woman's name] also thinks the same thing and said it a few minutes before he did. People don't like this. I've been taken aside after a meeting more than once and had it mansplained to me that I embarrassed the man by doing this. I have then calmly and confidently explained that the man had appropriated the views of the woman and expressed them as his own, and I didn't feel that was right.

Sometimes it is a man who calls bro-propriation out. I love these moments so much. They're rare but they do happen. They let me know that things are changing in positive ways. I always follow up with these men after a meeting to note and acknowledge what they did, thank them and let them know their actions are making a positive difference.

Putting forward a promotion application with attitude

In Chapter Two, I told you about the American study of online male and female teachers[20]. They could not be seen or heard by students and both taught a class as themselves, and a second class while pretending to be the opposite gender to their own. The performance of the male teacher pretending to be a woman got poorer evaluations than when the students knew he was a man. The female teacher scored higher when the students thought she was a man than when she revealed she was a woman. If you are an academic who teaches, I would suggest you consider putting forward an argument in your next promotion application, based on the evidence from this and numerous other similar studies, around the need for the panel to consider the evidence that you are being disadvantaged in your teaching evaluations compared to male colleagues. If you're not promoted, ask how the evidence that women receive lower teaching ratings than men was considered by the panel.

Either that, or buy a false moustache, change your name to a gender-non-specific 'Sam' or 'Chris', start wearing a three-piece suit and tie to class and try to lower your voice an octave or three. As I sometimes joke with female colleagues, if we all wore false moustaches, we might just get taken more seriously and we'd probably be running the place in no time. I'm only half joking.

Handling the style conversation with attitude

In Chapter One, I mentioned the importance of getting your style 'right' as a woman and 'the style conversation' that most senior women I know have had.

My most memorable style conversation was with an outsourced coach, appointed to work with me while I was a senior executive to address my terrible style problem. The feedback, from my mostly male colleagues, was that I had too much emphasis on achievement and results, was too direct and needed to adopt a softer style. It was decided that I needed to adopt less of a 'directive' and more of a 'coaching' approach to my leadership.

I was annoyed about this feedback and the decision that I needed to be more 'coach-like', partly because I am a qualified and registered psychologist. I have been registered for 23 years. Psychologists are educated and trained to help people to improve their lives, by listening to and empathising with them and then facilitating – or dare I say, *coaching* – them toward different thinking and behaviour. I was also annoyed because my PhD is *in coaching*, specifically coaching *in an academic context*. My coaching work has been published in refereed articles, and cited and implemented all over the world.

I was also annoyed because one of the most frequent areas I receive unsolicited feedback from people I work with is about my high-quality coaching and mentoring. Scores of women in particular have told me that my coaching of them has directly contributed to their success. But I digress, boasting about how fabulous I am (probably not advisable, especially as I'm not wearing my false moustache today).

I completed my style improvement coaching program (on how to be better at coaching) with my appointed coach. While I was doing the same, I worked out (from his boasting around the place about it) who had given the loudest and most negative feedback about my terrible style. Let's call him Tim. I reflected on what Tim was doing, consulted some of my mentors, asked HR for advice, carefully considered my options and, on the basis of all of that, I adopted a calm and working smarter attitude. I distanced myself from Tim and stopped communicating with him, except when there were witnesses present. At my next performance review several months later, my line manager commended me on my improved style. He singled out my significantly improved relationship with Tim as evidence that the coaching I had undertaken to be more coach-y (my word, not his) had worked very well indeed. (Tim went back to swanning around the place being unaccountable, not meeting his targets and annoying lots of people. *C'est la vie*.)

Recently, a female colleague told me she'd experienced the style conversation. Her line manager had asked her to reflect on her style and to think about what she thought her style *was now*, what she thought it *might be* and how she could be *assisted to adopt the style she wanted to adopt in the future* (my emphasis). My colleague is comfortable with her style – including in the past, present and future – and wondered aloud to me about why she should waste time thinking about her style when there were more important things to be getting on with.

I've counselled countless women about this inevitable style conversation. If you're a woman on the way up and you haven't had this conversation yet, the odds are that it's coming. I'd recommend adopting a carefully chosen attitude and then asking the person who has instigated this conversation whether they think the current conversation is gendered. If not, ask them to tell you (anonymously, of course) about the recent times they've had the same sort of style conversation with men, and what those men's reactions were to being asked to adjust their style. Just two or three stories of men's reactions to the style conversation that they can recall from the recent past.

Adopting unhelpful attitudes

My experiences and observations over my three decades in Australian universities have taught me that if you don't carefully adopt a particular attitude or attitudes, you are likely to be surprised by things that happen to you in your career. This surprise – or being caught off-guard – might lead to you reacting or responding in ways that do not serve you well.

For example, I have often chaired promotion panels and, as chair, I offer to meet with unsuccessful candidates if they would like feedback about how to improve their application (and therefore their odds of being promoted). Adopting an attitude of fury and outrage for this meeting will not help you. At the very least, it might obscure your ability to listen to the feedback being offered to you. Adopting a threatening attitude towards the chair, including threatening legal action if the decision about your promotion is not reversed, will also not be helpful to you. Being angry about the outcome is one thing but be careful about that angry attitude tipping over into an attitude that may not help you take the action you need to take to advance.

Choosing and applying attitudes

The examples and application of these attitudes provided in this section are by no means exhaustive. There are many other attitudes to adopt in addition to those described here. The number of personal circumstances and situations in which you might find yourself are endless. The point of this section is to prompt you to think strategically about how you are going to go about tackling sexism as it impacts you. You can read and consider the examples in this chapter in a number of ways:

- You can think about what sorts of attitudes best suit your personality and temperament.
- You can think about them in light of experiences you have had and that you have observed.
- You can consider them in relation to your personal circumstances and plans.

You might think that the detailed advice to carefully consider and adopt particular attitudes is a lot of emphasis on one aspect of navigating sexism. You are right. But my experience has taught me that women not being prepared and not having thought in advance about how to manage challenges puts them at a disadvantage. I would like to help you avoid that disadvantage – because goodness knows you have enough of those already as a woman.

Start thinking about saying no and being bad at housework

The final piece of advice in this chapter is about your attitudes to requests and to expectations around housework. Specifically, I suggest you start *thinking about* saying no and about being a bad housewife.

All day, most days, we are fielding requests. The requests are big and small, formal and informal, welcome and not. They're from senior executives, line managers, colleagues, students, funding bodies, external stakeholders, family, friends, acquaintances and, increasingly, complete strangers who make it through our message filtering systems. The requests are via every channel imaginable – work and personal email, text, WhatsApp, Twitter, LinkedIn, Zoom, phone and in person, just to name a few. If you stop to observe how many times a week you are asked for something, you would be forgiven for weeping. There are simply not enough hours available for you to focus on what counts *and* say yes to all of these asks.

Women are, more often than not, people pleasers. We are socialised to be – and rewarded for being – nice and nurturing. We often say yes. The problem with this is that many of the things we are asked to – and agree to – do will not help us advance in academia. It is time for you to start thinking about saying no. Continuing to agree to every request made of you will hold you back in academia. Saying no will enable you to protect your time as well as your energy and goodwill. You can then use these finite resources on the things that matter and on beating the odds.

Warren Buffet famously said, 'Successful people say no to almost everything.' Saying no is hard. Being raised to be a 'good girl' and a people pleaser, as most women are – coupled with being implicitly and unconsciously expected to continue this behaviour in the workplace – makes it harder for women to say no. I know it is not always possible to say no. There are certain expectations of you as an employee, and sometimes the only appropriate or professional response is 'yes'. But sometimes it is possible to say no, if you think about it carefully. I'll talk more about how to say no in later chapters. For now, I'd like you to *think about* what you could possibly say no to doing.

As women, we are also generally expected to take on the bulk of housework chores. The 2020 gender parity report from the World Economic Forum[21] states that there is no country in the world in which men spend the same amount of time on unpaid work as women. In countries where the ratio is lowest, it is still 2:1.

This expectation applies at home and at work. Doing housework at home and in our institutions uses up our precious time, energy and goodwill. We're

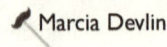
Marcia Devlin

often told we are so good at housework and that is why we keep being asked and expected to do it. By agreeing to do more housework because we are so good at it, we are participating in a ruse. It is time for you to start *thinking about* being bad at housework.

We all know people (usually, but not always, males) who are terrible at housework. They 'don't see' dirt, they 'don't notice' when the dishwasher needs emptying, they 'can't find' the mop (despite it being where it always is) and their 'folding' of clothes looks like it was undertaken by a drunk toddler. They are so bad at housework that it is easier and quicker to just do it all yourself (or pay for a cleaner). But women aren't born being good at housework. We are socialised – and reinforced – into doing most of it. Practice makes us better. We get very good at it indeed. Others around us then soon learn that if they do chores badly, they will eventually have the chores taken off them. It's time to start thinking carefully about this ruse, and the fact that you are complicit in it.

Start thinking about doing the housework at home less well. What if you didn't leave everything completely shiny and perfect for others to mess up? Think about it. What would happen if you stopped doing housework altogether, if only for a short time? I tried this once. It was a long time ago and before children, so it was doable in many ways. It was so much fun. I was working two hospitality jobs in split shifts and was rarely home, so it was relatively easy to ignore the mess and dirt. The flat quickly fell into complete disarray. There were clothes all over the floor. It got dusty. There were dishes piled in the sink. The kitchen floor was sticky. There were flies! The bathroom was a disgrace. It was so bad that my – until then oblivious – husband *noticed.* He tentatively asked me if I was OK. I smiled and said I'd never been better. A week or so later, he said, 'You know I didn't really notice how much housework you did until you stopped doing it.' Bingo. We then put up a roster and split the housework tasks 50/50. I've never looked back. *Think about it* – that's all I'm asking.

I'd also like you to start thinking about doing the housework at work less well. Institutional housework includes:
- being responsible for units of study with large enrolments – particularly with new first-year students who often need significant extra care and attention;
- coordinating large numbers of sessional staff and being their point of contact and support;
- teaching the same basic unit of study teaching period after teaching period after teaching period;

- taking multiple tutorials of the same unit of study during a teaching period;
- marking large numbers of the same assignment, again and again;
- taking the notes in staff meetings;
- organising birthday/farewell/whatever-the-occasion morning teas and other social events;
- washing up.

Such activities are necessary and important. Some of them are at the heart of academia and of collegiality. Many women are told they are *so good* at, for example, looking after first-year students, or managing the sessional staff. But such activities, critical as they are, do not and will not help you advance – particularly if you keep doing them year after year after year. And as one colleague has pointed out to me, *'They only add one line to your CV whereas doing different things adds multiple lines.'* What would happen if you stopped being so good at this work? What would be the impact? How might you proactively mitigate the worst of the impact (particularly on students) so you can stop putting so much of your time, energy and goodwill into this institutional housework? Just think about it.

It is hard to make the killer point in a meeting when you are busy doing other things.

Responsibility for institutional housework falls disproportionately on the shoulders of women. Adam Grant and Sheryl Sandberg wrote about institutional housework in an article humorously titled, 'Madam CEO – Get Me a Coffee'[22]. In it, the authors talk about expectations around 'office housework' – things like taking the notes in meetings – that are often placed on women. I have experienced this expectation directly, including while I was a university senior vice-president. I also sat in a meeting in 2019 where there were 21 attendees and only two of us were women – me as senior vice-president and the female notetaker (who was a PhD student offered the unpaid 'opportunity' to attend the meeting and take the notes). As Grant and Sandberg point out, these activities don't just use up our valuable time, they also contribute to us missing out on opportunities. As they point out, it is hard to make the killer point in a meeting when you are busy doing other things.

Grant and Sandberg point to the expectations of women to do office housework that has limited or no reward professionally for them. They

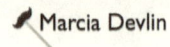
Marcia Devlin

highlight the gendered stereotypes we have of women to be nurturing and 'communal' and men to be ambitious and results-oriented, and argue that women help more in the workplace but benefit less from doing so. I'm asking you to think about this.

You might think you have no choice in relation to institutional housework – you have to do what your supervisor asks you to do. You might think that doing some of this work is your job, so you can't say no. You might be finding these sorts of roles and tasks rewarding and not want to say no to, or to be bad at, them. You might feel uncomfortable – or even scared by the thought of – saying no or doing your job at the less than perfect level at which you are accustomed to working. Of course, it's not always possible – or appropriate – to do your job or parts of your job badly. You are a professional and have a reputation to protect. But might it be possible to do some aspects of the institutional housework at a seven out of 10 standard, rather than your usual 10 out of 10 standard? What would happen if you tried that?

You might think you are too junior, or not confident enough, or that your students or your children will suffer if you try what I have suggested. I say poppycock. I'm only asking you to *think about it* at this stage. If you don't tell anyone what you're thinking, they won't even know.

Countless women have told me that getting 'stuck' doing low-level institutional housework tasks is one of the main contributors to their lack of – or slow speed of – advancement, compared to their male colleagues. Many have told me they wished they'd started saying no and being bad at housework earlier. Some have told me they regret being so good at low-level work because their reward was more of the same with the teeth-grindingly annoying justification, 'But you are just *so good* at this work.'

Write or type a list of 10 things that you could possibly say no to or stop doing, or could do at a seven out of 10 level for a little while. Include housework at home and at work. Don't filter, just brainstorm without judgement. Put them somewhere you can see and reflect on them.

I'm only asking you to *think about* saying no and being bad at some aspects of housework at home and at work – if only as a fantasy that you can enjoy. Thinking about this will help you get used to and become more comfortable with the idea and to be less scared about it. If you are able to put any of your thinking into practice, all the better. You will save time, energy and goodwill that can be channelled into focusing on your advancement.

Go on – think about it.

Conclusion

In this chapter I've covered the necessary quest of choosing an appropriate set of attitudes. I've also asked you to start thinking about saying no and being bad at housework. I hope you will give your attitude a lot of thought. Your context is key. What will work best in your context? Think carefully about what you could not do, or do but not as well as usual.

You might be nervous about trying the things I have suggested in this chapter. The beauty of them is that they are almost all inside your head. I've asked you to think about what sort of attitude you want and need to have around navigating the sexism you are facing, and will continue to face. I've asked you to fantasise about saying no and being bad at housework so you conserve your precious time, energy and goodwill for more important things. They are only thoughts at this stage. You can try much of what I've suggested in this chapter with little risk – it is all private for now.

What's coming up?

Now that you have done the necessary thinking, the next chapter details how to take some action. I'll explain why you need a secret strategy, goals and plans if you want to succeed in academia as a woman. And why you have to start actually saying no and being bad at housework.

CHAPTER FOUR

Prepare a Secret Strategy

Learning to strategise

Women in Australian universities don't expect to find obstacles in their career path in academia. They assume they will advance as they wish to. Those that have children assume they may take a little time off to have and raise children but they will return to 'normality' afterwards. Those who assume fairness and equality in universities are therefore often surprised and disappointed when their careers hit roadblocks and their advancement is slower than they had anticipated or would like.

Some women have a 'moment' where they notice that the blokes have most of the professorial appointments and leadership positions, and they begin to wonder what happened. I was one of these women. I looked around my department one day and saw that there were no women above senior lecturer level and the only professors were men. I mentioned it to the head of department and he got angry and defensive.

I started to focus on strategising and planning ahead. I learnt to define my success, to set goals related to my definition of success, and to methodically work my way toward achieving those goals. I learnt to proactively plan around my children and their likely needs at various stages of development. I also learnt to recalibrate when things changed or unexpected things happened. I learnt to take up some opportunities and pass on others. I learnt to move on when things weren't working out in a particular role or at a particular institution. I've now worked with scores of female academic and professional staff who have learnt the same things. Those of us who learn to strategise and plan, learn not only to survive but also to thrive in academia.

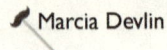

Without a carefully executed strategy designed to help you beat the odds, you are likely to become a statistic. Without carefully planning for, and proactively anticipating and managing, the obstacles that will hold you back as a female in academia, you will probably end up as one of the majority of women at the lower levels of academia. I have helped scores of women to successfully strategise and plan their careers – and moves within their careers. I have also watched many women who relied on trusting the system and hoping their significant contributions and hard work would be noticed and rewarded. In my experience, those with a strategy and a plan fare far better. While nothing is guaranteed and sexism is not going away any time soon, by designing and preparing a strategy to guide and motivate you, you will be better positioned to beat the odds.

Being strategic means identifying goals and the actions you can take to meet those goals.

A warning: This chapter is not for the faint-hearted. It requires you to make some commitments and take some actions toward your success. It also points out – again – the need to carefully navigate the gendered expectations of you. Get ready – having carefully thought about the attitudes you will adopt and the ways you will say no, including to housework, at the end of the last chapter, you're now about to start the process of really beating the odds.

Preparing a strategy for your advancement essentially means deciding where to put your focus and resources. It also means preparing a detailed plan of action for achieving success – whatever that means for you. Being strategic means identifying goals and the actions you can take to meet those goals. You must also utilise all of the resources available to you, to help you take all the actions necessary to meet your goals.

You may think the future is too uncertain to strategise or plan for in any detailed or helpful way. You are both right and wrong. The future is uncertain, and 2020, of all years, taught us all so much about not being able to predict the future with any certainty. But a good strategy is at a level where it can still be useful, even when shifts as large as a global pandemic come along. As a good strategist, you will have regular 'review and revise' actions as part of your repertoire, so you can make sure that your strategy is always working for you.

It is true that, no matter how good a strategy may be, reality can get in the way of the best-laid plans. It's also true that goals can change over time, and something you may think that you want to focus on at one period in your life becomes less important at a later period. But a good strategist knows when to refresh her strategy to accommodate changes, and when to take a breather.

The secret bit

When describing a female university colleague, someone once said to me, 'She's *very strategic.* She'll do *anything* to get ahead.' In case you are wondering, this was not a compliment. Being described as strategic is rarely a compliment for a woman. In this chapter, I will tell you about how to be strategic if you want to beat the odds. Because you are a woman, being strategic will probably not be well perceived by others. They will unconsciously expect you to be focused on the success of others, not yourself. If you take the advice I offer in this chapter, it might be wise to keep the fact that you are being strategic about your career a secret. I'm serious.

Defining success

When I was in my late 20s, and before I had children, I undertook a life-changing exercise called *The Funeral Exercise.* A female pro vice-chancellor at my university ran a professional development day for women interested in progressing their careers, and *The Funeral Exercise* was the icebreaker. You have to imagine you are dead (bear with me here), you are lying in your coffin at your funeral and you can hear what people are saying about you. We were asked to draw a picture of ourselves in our own coffin at our funeral. Then, next to that picture, we were asked to write down three headings: 'Family', 'Friends' and 'Colleagues'. Underneath each of the three headings, we were asked to write a list of words that each group would use to describe us at the end of our life. Stop here for a few minutes and give this a go. Look at what the three lists say. Reflecting on these lists might help you with your strategy and plans.

When I completed this exercise, and after taking just a few moments out to reflect on my life, I felt a bit worried. The lists for the three groups of people were almost identical and they all said things like 'career-oriented', 'work-focused', 'dedicated to her job' and not much else. If I kept going the way I was headed, I was on track to end up with a pretty boring, limited, one-track life with my only real interest being in my job – and possibly divorced and with no friends.

I confronted the fact that my life was pretty one-dimensional and that that wasn't what I wanted it to be. It is not an exaggeration to say that doing this exercise changed my life. By the end of the full-day workshop, having been firmly committed to not having children, despite my husband's desires to be a father, I had decided now was a good time to start a family. I'm not sure that was the objective for the female PVC who ran the development day, but I owe her a great debt. You can only imagine my red-blooded husband's surprise (and delight) when I got home, he asked how the course went and I said, 'Great. Let's talk about it in the bedroom.'

Our eldest son, Finn, was born about 18 months later and Aengus followed just under two years after that. Since doing *The Funeral Exercise*, and up until pretty recently, I've planned and arranged my career and life around the needs of Finn and Aengus. I value my role as a mother above any other. My choice to have my children and to play a significant, hands-on part in raising them while continuing to have and build a career meant I had to strategise, think ahead, and plan and re-plan constantly. I have taken advantage of all opportunities offered to me through maternity leave – part-time work, flexible hours, contracts, casual work, carer's leave and so on. I stayed at Level B for more than 12 years so I could be as good a mother as I could possibly be. This is a core value for me and a central part of my definition of success.

Your values and definition of success will guide your strategy and, in particular, your goal setting, which we discuss in a moment. You will need to revisit and refine your definition – and goals – periodically throughout your life and career. For example, when I left one university to take up a promotion at another, I recalibrated my definition of success slightly. When I told Aengus, who was nine years old at the time, about the upcoming move, he asked apprehensively whether this change meant that I wouldn't be able to pick him up straight after school on Tuesdays. Tuesday afternoons were a special time for both of us. I took Aengus to footy training and then helped out, running the warm-up session for a bunch of 8 and 9 year olds. It was a highlight of my week (and obviously important to Aengus as well).

So, for that phase of my life, I defined success as surviving a new position with high expectations and responsibilities, while still being able to pick Aengus up straight after school on Tuesdays. I will add that after the warm-up, I went back to the car and took out my laptop. I spent that quiet, uninterrupted time while Aengus was training under his coach answering emails from the day and working on papers I was writing at the time.

In order to be successful, you need to understand how *you* define success. Success means something different to each and every one of us.

You are reading this book because you want to be successful in academia. This is a relatively straightforward goal if you have nothing else in your life. But we all have other things in our lives besides advancing at work – and if not, we probably should have. Ask yourself, 'What does success look like in my career and life?' so that you can guide your limited time, effort and resources appropriately.

At another point in my career progression, I found success in taking a demotion and an internal move within my institution. I was not enjoying – nor thriving in – the role I held. In fact, I was having difficulty surviving while trying to manage one of the most difficult colleagues I have ever had reporting to me. I had started to become ill with stress and decided that putting my wellbeing at ongoing risk for the sake of my career was not worth the cost. I value my health and wellbeing and defined success at that time along the lines of 'still having a job in academia and not having a nervous breakdown'. I'm serious. And honestly, if I lived that time over, I would make the same decision to take a demotion to escape from the toxic environment I was in.

I'm not the only woman who has moved down – or across – to live her values and find her version of success. Women's academic and professional careers are often complex and non-linear, and I know many female colleagues who have made unusual moves to broaden their experience, or escape a poor leader or a bad environment – or both. While I don't recommend taking a demotion *per se*, do whatever works for you at the time to ensure you do not compromise your values and that you do meet your definition of success.

You may have a simple definition of success; for example, to reach the level of professor. Great! Your work is done, in terms of defining what success looks like for you. But are there any other elements of success for you? Would you like to have harmonious working relationships with those closest to you? Would you like to be warmly admired across the world for the quality of your work? Would you like to have a good level of fitness and/ or fun in your personal life? A family with whom you are deeply connected? Time to read some of the great novels? Any other elements of a whole life? If so, your strategy and plan can help ensure that you don't achieve one goal, or one part of your definition of success, at the cost of others. You might prefer not to define precisely what success might look like in the future and instead leave your options open. That's OK too – but having some general or broad goals will help you strategise and plan your advancement in ways that anticipate and navigate the odds against you.

You might be thinking about all the elements of life and careers over which we have limited or no influence and wondering how to define success in such a context. Acknowledge what you already know – that you can only influence and control certain aspects of your life. Focus on the aspects that you can influence or control and set some goals around these. Make them realistic in your context, but don't be afraid to be ambitious as well. Just don't tell anyone about the ambition bit – remember, it's not ladylike.

Think about what success really means for you right now. I use 'The Seven Fs'[23] to help me do this:

1. Family
2. Friends
3. Fun
4. Fitness (physical and mental)
5. Faith (principles and/or personal philosophy; values)
6. Formal (and informal) learning
7. Finances (work)

Some versions swap out some of the Fs; for example, one I have seen swaps 'Formal learning' for 'Future'. Whatever the makeup of the seven, I try to have both definitions of success and goals in each of these areas. There are a few variations online and you can find these easily with your search engine. Maybe this, or another framework, will help you determine what you value and how you define success. It doesn't matter how you do this – what matters is that you determine what success means for you and revisit your understanding from time to time to make sure it is still fit for your purpose and serving you well.

Finally, it is worth articulating what is implicit in all of the above and what can feel obvious – that your definition of success must align with your values. If there is little or no alignment, you will quickly come to grief and have to redefine.

The next step after defining success is setting goals related to this definition.

Setting (strategic) goals

The basis of a good advancement strategy is clarity about how you define success. For the purposes of your professional advancement, narrow in on clear goals or outcomes in that arena. To develop these, ask yourself questions like, 'What do I want my professional contribution to be?' and 'What would I like to be known for?' These questions can help you clarify your professional purpose, or primary professional purpose – at least right now. This purpose can morph and change over time as your expertise develops and your interests change. Your primary professional purpose underpins your goals, which are the specific ways in which you will meet this purpose.

My career has focused variously on student learning, teaching quality, plagiarism, effectively supporting disadvantaged students, digital education, leadership, women in leadership and several other themes. At one time, I defined my professional purpose around student retention and success. Specifically, my primary professional purpose at the time was to make a difference to policy and practice in student retention and success in Australia. Over a period of years, I:

- created and took up an opportunity to write a university-wide student retention and success strategy;
- successfully led the implementation of that strategy;
- advised other universities on the development of their own strategies;
- sought and won research funds and undertook research in this area;
- wrote and published research reports, journal articles, chapters and popular media articles on the topic;
- gave keynote addresses on this topic; and
- spoke to a government expert panel on this topic to inform policy.

I feel that I achieved that purpose – through achieving many related goals – as far as I was able to within my power at the time. I eventually moved on to another primary purpose.

Write your purpose down and put it somewhere you can see it every day.

It is helpful, as an ambitious woman, to spend time working out your primary professional purpose to guide your goal setting. Clarity around your purpose will also help guide your decision-making and efforts. Write your purpose down and put it somewhere you can see it every day (but others can't – it's a secret for now). Reflect on it, refine and tweak it whenever you wish to. Then commit to this purpose – at least for now. This will help you strategise, set your goals and plan how you will achieve them. Remember, you can change your purpose (and almost certainly will), so you are not necessarily making a career-long commitment.

With your broad, current professional purpose clarified, ask yourself questions like, 'What, specifically, do I want to achieve within this purpose?', 'What outcomes would let me know that I am meeting my aims and/or

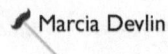
Marcia Devlin

purpose(s)?' and, 'At the end of my career, what would I like people to say about me and my contributions related to this purpose?' Then note these draft goals somewhere handy (and secret). We're going to refer to them as you work your way through this chapter. You will need to work out where you are heading and why so that you can purposefully navigate your way towards that destination. Remember, these are just your draft goals for now – you can (and will) add to and change them at any time.

Setting goals is only so useful. You have to commit to them and put them into action. We'll talk about that in the rest of the chapter. This might feel like articulating your professional purpose and setting goals aligned with this and your values is a bit complex or over the top. You may not yet know what your primary professional purpose is, or be struggling to articulate it. If so, you might want to flick back and have a look at the example I gave you of my purpose at one point. Is there something along those lines that would inspire you? If not, that's fine – just keep your goal setting simple. A dot-point list of goals is absolutely fine. The key thing is that you have goals. Without them, you do not have a clear direction and this puts you at risk of a lack of focus and of poor decision-making about your career choices.

You may feel you are too busy to set goals, or that you are just not comfortable doing this sort of thing. Or that goal setting is a bit old fashioned or passé. I'd say, take a big breath and give it a go anyway. You may never have thought about applying this kind of business strategy to your life. But it works for business so why not for you? Having a clear definition of what success means to you and articulating goals related to that definition will be worth your time and be beneficial to you.

If you've defined what success means for you, clarified your primary professional purpose and drafted some goals, as I've suggested above, you've already started strategising and planning. You're well on your way, so you may as well keep going and see what happens.

Making plans

I don't know who said 'A goal without a plan is just a dream,' but I agree with her. If you are reading this book, one of your goals is to advance in academia. Whether that is to advance to lecturer, manager, professor, vice-chancellor or something in between, without a plan, you're less likely to reach your goal(s). Whatever they are, your goals will be linked to your primary professional purpose and your broader definition of success. As one changes, so does the other. Women I have mentored and coached have told me that this is one of the most useful pieces of advice I have offered them – that, and reminding the ones with children that you can have it all, but maybe not all at the same time. We will come back to this.

> *When a woman is noticed and 'lifted up' in some way, this 'kindness' often comes with strings.*

I have worked with scores of women who did not have a strategy or plan for their career. They have assumed and trusted that their hard work, effort and strong academic and/or professional citizenry will be rewarded with recognition, including through promotion and being offered attractive opportunities. More than a few have had a secret fantasy that 'someone' will notice them and their contributions and/or good character, and then either mentor, sponsor, rescue and/or help them in some other way to advance. I'm sorry to tell you that this is extremely rare. When a woman is noticed and 'lifted up' in some way, this 'kindness' often comes with strings. In the worst cases, I know of women who have been helped by a senior male colleague who then expects sexual favours in return. I know of other cases where women are deliberately given the 'opportunity' to lead in what turns out to be an extremely difficult situation or environment with little chance of success, and the woman is then blamed for the inevitable failure. This is a well-known phenomenon called 'the glass cliff' (and I talk more about this in Chapter Seven). In less shocking cases, I know of women who have been helped by senior male and female colleagues and then expected to undertake difficult (sometimes impossible), dull and/or repetitive work that no-one else wants – which uses up enormous amounts of their effort, energy and goodwill and gives them little or no advantage.

A strategy and/or plan is something that is within your control, unlike the poor behaviour of others described above. While a plan will not overcome the poor behaviour of those with more power than you, a plan will help guide your decision-making and assess potential opportunities against your personal definition of success, your goals and your timelines. But plans are only so useful. For example, we can't possibly know all the future factors that will impact on our success or progress. Having plans, however, will more often help you than not. It is, therefore, worth the small amount of effort required to make plans. Having plans can also help with having a sense of agency in the face of larger forces and systems.

It is also true that not everything can be helped by a plan. Life throws curve balls at us all and these often come at inopportune times – if there is ever an opportune time. To improve on the work of poet Robert Burns, the best-laid plans of mice and women oft go awry. I don't know much about the mice, but for the women life plans are often interrupted by caring responsibilities, relationship matters and health issues. Mine certainly have been.

Sometimes, goals have to be put aside for a time while we deal with more important things – and that's fine. You can always park a plan and revisit it when you are ready again.

Examples of how to plan

You can choose from countless ways to plan. Here are a few examples of the way I plan. Feel free to use these – or, equally, to use any other method. Your search engine will offer dozens of approaches and templates. What matters is that you plan to help you beat the odds.

10-year plan

Start your planning with a 10-year plan. Take a piece of paper or a blank document on your computer. Draw or insert a table with 11 rows (the heading row plus one row each for 10 years) and enough columns to include:

- the year;
- a column for each of your children; and
- at least two more columns.

I have two children and we have extensive family overseas who we try to meet up with about every two to three years. It's a big deal and we need to plan for this trip and coordinate up to 19 people to meet at an agreed location where none of us live, which caters to all ages and needs across three generations. The meet up also has to take into account kids' school levels and breaks and adult work commitments. It takes about two years to organise each meetup. Below is an excerpt from my 10-year plan from 2011. In it, I list the ages and school/education years of each of my sons, and major work goals and family considerations for each year. See Table 13.

Prepare a Secret Strategy

Table 13: An excerpt from my 10-year plan from 2011

Year	Finn	Aengus	Work goal	Personal
2011	15 Year 9	13 Year 7	Contract ends 2012 – start looking	Aengus transition year
2012	16 Year 10	14 Year 8	Find next role	
2013	17 Year 11	15 Year 9	Senior role?	Finn starts VCE
2014	18 Year 12	16 Year 10	Senior role?	No overseas family meet up (Finn Yr 12)
2015	19 First year uni	17 Year 11	PVC? Board training; Seek board role	Aengus starts VCE
2016	20 Second year uni	18 Year 12	PVC? Gain board experience	No overseas family meet up (Aengus year 12)
2017	21 Third year uni	19 First year uni	PVC? Gain board experience MBA?	Overseas family meet up
2018...				
2019...				

The plan was just that. Things worked out differently in real life after I wrote this plan. For example, Finn changed schools – twice – in 2011. In 2014, I unexpectedly became a deputy vice-chancellor. Whoops. The role was at a regional location and my office was two hours' drive from my home. It was not sensible, nor safe, to spend four hours a day commuting. With detailed arrangements and strong encouragement and support from my husband in place, I spent part of each week between 2014 and 2017 living apart from my family and nearer to work.

In 2016, Aengus became unwell and spent a lot of time in hospital during his final year of school. He needed a lot of support from my husband and I to recover from his serious illness and to make up for having missed more than two months of school. As a result, I didn't gain the board experience I planned to gain that year. In 2017, I'd had enough of the challenges of being apart from my family and I left my regional deputy vice-chancellor role to be closer to home. I decided not to start the MBA I had planned. As things changed, I redid the plan – what is presented above is just one version.

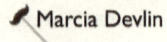
Marcia Devlin

You don't know exactly what is going to happen in life or at work. But in my case, planning for the years that the kids would need particular stability informed my decision-making about work and personal matters – as far as was possible. The 10-year plan (and all plans, ideally) need to be reviewed regularly and updated as circumstances and goals change. I look at mine a few times a year and more often if there are major changes that were not anticipated.

One-year plan

Once you have given the 10-year plan a try, I suggest a more detailed plan that is focused on your work goals. Here is an excerpt from a fictional plan that is focused on the goal of 'Get promoted next year'.

Table 14: An excerpt from a fictional one-year plan

Strategy	Actions	Timeline	Notes	3 month review
Strategy 1: Raise my profile*	Review digital profiles of 8 senior women	End of January		
	Contact media office and arrange media training	End of January		
	Draft a digital profile	Early February		
	Arrange for professional photographs	Early February		
	Finalise digital profile and ask IT to upload	End February		
	Create ResearchGate profile	End February		
	Make a list of colleagues with whom I want to engage (internal and external)	End February		
Strategy 2: ...				

* The importance of this strategy to getting promoted is explained in detail in Chapter Five.

Unlike the 10-year plan, which is high level and general, this one-year plan is focused and details the specific actions you will take – and by when. You can use the 'Notes' column to jot down weekly or fortnightly updates. I recommend a full review every three months to make sure you are on track and that the plan is still fit for your purpose. It's your plan, so you can change it if you wish.

You may not see the value in planning, especially down to a detailed level. You may have tried planning and seen that things didn't work out and now feel discouraged about planning. You don't have to take all the advice offered here. That said, throughout my career in universities, I have noticed that most successful women have formal plans or intuitively use planning to help them navigate their careers – particularly, but not only, if they have children. Personally, I certainly would not have reached senior vice-president and senior deputy vice-chancellor without a lot of planning and plans – constantly reviewed and revised as life and work unfolded. I'd suggest you give planning a try to see if there are any learnings or potential benefits for you in developing and trying to follow a plan. You can always give it away if you feel it's not helping you.

Start saying no and being bad at housework

In the previous chapter, I asked you to start *thinking about* saying no and being bad at housework. In this chapter, I'm asking you to start *taking action*. I simply cannot stress enough how much saying yes to so many requests and doing so much of the domestic and institutional housework contributes to gender inequity. I have mentioned the 'shoulds' previously. That there should be programs and commitments and change that ensures women have equal representation in senior roles and so on.

At a broader level, the World Economic Forum Gender Parity Report 2020[24] states that 'Without changing legislation and cultural/social attitudes towards the relative amount of time women spend on unpaid domestic work and care, the burden of household and care duties will not be rebalanced, a situation that will continue to undermine women's career opportunities.' Legislation and attitudes should change. But these 'shoulds' are outside your sphere of control and you can only have limited influence on them, if any. However, you have a lot more control and influence over how you choose to spend your limited time, energy and goodwill. Right now, if you are a typical woman, you are spending much of these limited resources on doing what is asked of you and on domestic and institutional housework. You are spending your resources on being a good girl. But these activities simply don't count

Marcia Devlin

for advancement in academia. Continuing to do them is contributing to holding back your advancement.

Saying no and being bad at housework is risky business. You will be challenging the gendered expectations of you. You may be seen as selfish. You may upset people. So you have a choice. You can keep doing what you're doing and wait for the 'shoulds' to materialise. Or you can choose to act now. My advice is to do both. Act now, while you wait for the 'shoulds' to come later. If you want to beat the odds in academia, it's time for you to start saying no and being bad at housework.

Start saying no

Personally, I find it very hard to say no. I'd love to say no more but I often feel compelled to say yes. For example, while I have been writing this chapter, I met someone I didn't want to meet and spent *hours* with them when I would much rather have been doing something else. Yet I couldn't say no to this person because I didn't want her to think badly of me.

If you're like me, you might worry about disappointing someone or hurting their feelings. You might be worried about making someone powerful angry, appearing rude or, worst of all, being seen as selfish. We know what happened to poor Heidi and she didn't even refuse a request. You may worry about the repercussions of saying no – many women in universities do, and sometimes with good reason. There might be payback and it's usually a bitch. I have suffered payback for declining 'offers' to do yet another thing on top of an already impossible workload. Some of these paybacks have had difficult personal and professional consequences – which is why I understand that you have to use your judgement about when to say no. When you do choose to say no, you need to do this carefully.

Writing in the *Harvard Business Review* about how to say no at work[25], Bruce Tuglan proposes first analysing the request that has been made of you. You can use your training and skills as an academic or professional critical thinker to unpack the request – the pros and cons, the likely benefits, the known costs, the likely repercussions of saying yes and of saying no, and so on – then make an evidence-based, informed decision.

If you do say no, Tuglan proposes delivering a 'well-reasoned' no. I've had some training in this. Immediately upon starting in a new executive role with a broad, wide and deep set of responsibilities, I was also concurrently placed on more than 20 university committees, for many of which I was the chair. Not surprisingly, I was having trouble coping with my workload. Rather than reduce my workload, my (male) line manager asked me to work with a coach to improve my performance. The coach helped me figure out some criteria for saying no to committee requests. These included proposing someone better suited or qualified to serve on the committee in my place, offering my seat to someone else as a useful development opportunity, and recommending to the line manager a different route to addressing the issue at hand instead of creating yet another committee. In desperation to reduce my workload, I also secretly drew up a plan for me to miss every third or fourth meeting of certain committees that I really didn't need to be at every single time, but couldn't delegate because my line manager wouldn't have approved.

In less complex circumstances, the 'no' message need only be short and simple. You don't need to give a long, detailed justification. You can try saying something like, 'I'm afraid I'm not able to take that on,' or, 'Unfortunately, I don't have time to do that with my current workload,' or the good old, 'No, thank you.' Be polite, but firm and direct. You can also try, 'Thanks for asking me but I'm afraid it's not convenient right now,' or, 'I'm sorry, but I can't help you this time.' If you're not ready for a clean 'no', or that is not appropriate for the situation, you might be able to try, 'Is there another unit/task I can help with instead? I've done this one for a few years now.'

The more you say no, the easier it will get and the less you will worry about it.

You could consider practising saying no – perhaps to insignificant things like being offered a drink at a friend's house, or to requests for small favours from family members. Try to remember that you are not a bad person, parent or friend if you say no. If you are struggling with saying a straight-out 'no' to something, you could consider offering a compromise in the meantime while you build your 'saying no' muscle. For example, you could say yes, but only for a limited time. Or you could suggest the task is shared between you and another colleague (perhaps a male at the same level or one level higher – the latter so you can 'learn from him').

Your time, effort and goodwill – not to mention your talent – are valuable. That's why you are often asked to do things. But they are also finite. You can't just endlessly agree to everything you are asked to do. As well as freeing up time to work on things that will matter for your advancement, saying no more often will free up time, effort and goodwill to spend on care for yourself – on being the best academic, professional, leader, colleague, friend, parent, family member and person.

 Marcia Devlin

Doing something new is hard. The more you say no, the easier it will get and the less you will worry about it. If you want to beat the odds – and I'm going to be blunt – it is time to start saying no.

Start being bad at housework

As well as saying no, the time has come to move on from just *thinking* about being bad at housework, to *actually* being bad at housework. I'll use cooking as one example of housework at home that usually falls to women.

On my second date with the man who is now my husband of 30 years, he served me dinner at his house. It was delicious. I asked him where he got the food, assuming the vegetarian curry, rice, poppadoms and chutney were from one of the local Indian restaurants nearby. He didn't understand the question. 'Where did I get it?' he repeated. 'Yeah, which Indian?' I asked. 'I made it myself,' he said. My eyes widened and I mentally checked off my other criteria for boyfriends at the time. Intelligent? Yep. Respectful? Yep. Handsome? Oh, yessiree. 'I'm going to marry you,' I thought to myself. I'd known him for less than two weeks. Honestly, choosing the life partner I did was the single most influential factor on my career success. My husband does all the cooking and has done so for three decades.

OK, I know I've lost some of you here, at least momentarily. I understand that I am very, very fortunate. I understand that cooking (and the related menu planning and shopping) take up a lot of time, energy and headspace – and this work is largely invisible and usually taken for granted by the people for whom you cook. If you are reading this book, you probably do the lion's share of the cooking for yourself and whoever lives with you. You might enjoy cooking (and menu planning and shopping), but I bet you also enjoy having someone else plan, shop and cook for you – if only from time to time.

If so, why don't you let someone else do that for you more often? Or insist on it? Why do you do all, or most, of this task every day, week, month and year? Is it because you've had the most practice and are, therefore, the best at it? Do others not cook at your house because you are so much better at cooking? A young woman I worked with recently told me that my suggestion to her that she and her live-in fiancé share the cooking equally was one of the best pieces of advice she had been given. The situation had arisen in their house – as it often does – where she was responsible for the bulk of the cooking. And, therefore, the planning and shopping for the cooking. Why? They both have two arms and two legs. Whether it's your partner, other adults you live with, friends or family you don't live with, or a restaurant or catering service, you could save time and energy (and possibly goodwill, depending on your feelings about cooking) by activating a different way of organising meals. Then you can use that time, energy and goodwill on the things that count for advancement in academia.

About 10 years ago, I sat next to a younger Level B colleague in a seminar at work. She was typing out a menu with suggested meals for her kids, carefully balancing protein with vegetables and so on. Particular preferences of each of her children were noted next to suggestions for meals. I asked what she was doing. She explained that she was going overseas for work for a couple of weeks, and that her husband was going to be looking after the kids while she was away. She went on to add that her husband didn't usually cook, didn't know what each of their children liked and disliked, and that he probably wouldn't be able to think of what to feed them in any case. So she had decided to make it easier for her husband and better for the kids by preparing menus for the two weeks.

There are many ways to look at this anecdote, which I'm certain happens around the country when female academics and professionals, who are also primary caregivers to children, step out of the home and away from the children for work. One is that this is a sad reflection on modern families. The other is that this young female academic had begun a process of greater sharing of responsibility for child rearing with her partner. I chose the latter of the two interpretations (while feeling grateful for being partnered with someone who loves to shop and cook).

This young colleague travelled overseas and, reportedly, no-one in her family starved to death in her absence. She later told me she had subsequently subscribed to a meal service where fresh meat and vegetables are delivered to your door weekly, with meal plans for use of the groceries that have been selected for you. She explained that the service removes the time and effort in meal planning, shopping and cooking. I didn't ask, but presumably hubby can read and follow menu/cooking instructions (he does run his own firm after all) and there was continued and perhaps greater sharing of meal responsibilities in their house following the engagement of that service. Years later, she told me she was travelling every week for work. Again, there were no reports of anyone dying of hunger at her place. I hope you will be pleased to hear that this still quite young colleague is now a professor.

Housework at work

I talked in the last chapter about being expected to do institutional housework at work because you are a woman. Ever seen a man wash the dishes after a work morning tea? Ignore me, I'm being ridiculous. What about seeing

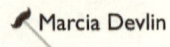
Marcia Devlin

a man clearing a few plates after a morning tea – into a pile for a woman to wash? And how much praise did he get when he did this? I'll bet it was more than the small group of women doing the bulk of the clean-up received collectively. We expect women to do this housework – and we are not kind when they don't. Grant and Sandberg argue that if a woman declines to help in the workplace, she is less liked. A man who declines is likely to be seen as 'busy', a woman who declines is 'selfish' and this is not good for her career advancement, as we discussed in Chapter Two.

Heijstra and colleagues argue that the fact that women carry the main responsibility for domestic and caring tasks at home follows them into the academic arena[26]. In their 2019 article, *Women professors and the academic housework trap*, Macfarlane and Burg find that female professors are more likely to emphasise the importance of academic citizenship – especially, but not only, through mentoring – compared to their male counterparts[27]. They suggest these findings are indicative of the ongoing effects of 'academic housework' in holding back the careers of academic women.

Noting that women are good at identifying the needs of others, Grant and Sandberg suggest that women turn that talent to place more focus and value instead on what *they themselves* need[28]. The risk here, of course, is the Heidi Effect – just by being a woman you are at risk of being seen as 'selfish'. This will obviously increase if you aren't seen to be helpful and doing the work expected of you. Grant and Sandberg also suggest that men step forward to take more responsibility for the office housework. I'll say that again. *It would be helpful if men stepped forward and did more of the office housework.*

As a woman, you could gently and carefully encourage men to do this. One time, at the end of taking the notes in an informal but regular meeting with other executive colleagues, I said, 'I'll type these notes up and send them around ahead of our next catch up. Maybe I can nominate Bill to take the notes at the next meeting so we can share the notetaking around?' I'm happy to report that when I made this suggestion, the world kept turning and civilisation as we know it did not collapse. Bill did give me a dirty look (I saw it, Bill) but life went on.

Remember the list of 10 things that you could possibly say no to or stop doing, or could do at a seven out of 10 level for a little while that I asked you to write or type out in Chapter Three? It's time to select a small number of these you can commit to. Now put them into action. Monitor how you go and how you feel for the next two weeks. Watch carefully and see if civilisation ends. If not, keep doing those things and consider adding a couple more to your list. Keep saying no and being a 7/10. If you want a stretch assignment, try being a 6/10 or even a 5/10. Try saying no and being bad at housework.

> *If you want to advance in academia, you'll need to carve out time.*

Sometimes, for a range of reasons, you might have to say yes when you really don't want to – and could – say no. Sometimes, you won't be able – or want – to give the bathroom a quick 'once over' rather than a deep and thorough clean. Sometimes there might be a potential benefit in saying yes. But remember, there are only 168 hours in a week and you'll need to spend some of them sleeping, grooming, caring for yourself and possibly others, participating in relationships, preparing and eating food, exercising, and otherwise living. That doesn't leave much time. If you want to advance in academia, you'll need to carve out time. Saying no and being bad at housework will help you find at least some of that time. Why not give it a try? I promise no-one will die as a result. Probably, no-one at home will notice the drop in cleaning standards (and if they do – they are welcome to take over responsibility). Most people at work won't notice a delay in responding to their message and will even forgive and may themselves follow up a non-response. It's time for you – and it's up to you – to take action.

Conclusion

I have explained to you the benefits of preparing a secret strategy and plans. You have defined success for yourself and you will revisit this definition as your life and career advance. You understand that, as a woman, you need to be covert about your ambition and about the fact that you are taking control of your career through developing a strategy and detailed plans. You understand that your time, energy and goodwill are precious – and you need to protect them and make careful choices about where to expend these finite resources.

You may feel like you would like to skip this chapter and ignore its advice. You might reasonably think that if I, as the author of this book, can't say no, how on earth can you? You might hate me for having a husband who cooks (you wouldn't be the first) and think I don't understand. You may just want to get onto the next chapter, which talks about how to get promoted and into a leadership position. But the current chapter has already started telling you how to get promoted and achieve leadership positions. You need

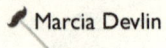

to pay attention to all you have just read. Remember Warren Buffet's words, 'Successful people say no to almost everything.'

This chapter lays the groundwork for the next one, so if you've skipped over or sped-read it, go back and read it carefully. If you've read it carefully but not taken the actions I've recommended around defining success, drafting goals, making plans, saying no and being bad at housework, I'd recommend taking those actions now. This chapter requires you to make some commitments and take some steps toward being successful. I've seen some women take these steps even mid-career, and seen enormous improvements. Spend a bit of time here – I promise it will be a useful investment in your future and will help you advance in academia.

What's coming up?

The next chapter talks about doing more of what matters – and less of what doesn't – for success in a university setting. It focuses on what matters for advancement in academia. If you have followed the advice in the current chapter, you are ready for the next one.

CHAPTER FIVE

Do More of What Counts – and Less of What Doesn't

Get specific

By now, you will have defined what success means for you and have started developing a strategy, plan and goals. You need to focus on specific aspects of your work that are relevant for your advancement and – in particular in this chapter – academic promotion. If you are a professional staff member, most of the chapter is relevant to you, but you will probably skip over the bits about teaching and research. Don't miss the bits on upping your profile, watching out for traps and saying no. In this chapter I make some recommendations to which women need to particularly pay attention, whatever sort of appointment they have.

To advance in academia or any field, you need to do more of the things that are valued by decision-makers. This is true whether you are a man or a woman. But, over my time in universities, I've noticed some things that women are better at doing and are not so good at doing. This chapter primarily focuses on the latter. This includes having a high profile, doing more of the things that count for promotion and avoiding more of the things that don't count for promotion.

To be promoted, you have to meet or exceed certain criteria. You also have to convince the members of the promotion panel that you have sufficient quantities of high-quality evidence to back your claims. This chapter talks about some of the key things in these quests. There is much for you to do, especially if you are a woman who is expected to be a good girl and take care of housework at home and at work. You will need even more advice and prompting on saying no and becoming worse at housework.

Up your profile

To avoid being overlooked and to be sure that you are on the radar of decision-makers, you need to make sure people know who you are and the value you add. The best way to do this is to raise your profile.

A high – or strong – profile can help you get recruited and/or promoted. Technically, being known to the selection or promotion panel members is not a criterion for a successful application. But, from my firsthand experience of sitting on and chairing hundreds of recruitment and promotion panels, it can be beneficial to your chances as an applicant to be known to one or more panel members. Hearing a firsthand account of the impact of a candidate's work from a panel member reinforces claims made in an application and can be powerful – particularly when the decision is a close call. While your record and achievements can – and must – speak for themselves in a promotion application, you can also assist your odds by being known for the work you do, the impact that work has and the value you and your work will bring, or already bring, to an institution.

Having a profile assists you in other ways too. Opportunities that contribute to your progress in academia – in interim, acting or ongoing leadership positions – are not always offered through a merit-based promotion or recruitment process. Having a high internal profile at your own institution can put you on the radar of decision-makers when *ad hoc* opportunities arise.

> *A high – or strong – profile can help you get recruited and/or promoted.*

The value of a positive internal profile can be seen in the movement of 15 vice-chancellors in 2020, which I referred to in Chapter One. Of the 11 males appointed as vice-chancellors during 2020, six of them – or 55 percent – were internal candidates from the same institution. Three of the six moved up within their organisation to become the next permanent vice-chancellor. Another three are internal candidates acting/interim in the role of vice-chancellor while the formal recruitment takes place. Those six men did not hide their lights under any bushels before they were elevated to the most senior role in their institution. They were on the radar of the council who made the decision to appoint them. See Table 15.

Table 15: Australian vice-chancellors appointed in 2020, by gender and internal/external, as at February, 2021

University	Female	Male	Internal appointment
Australian Catholic		√	√
Charles Darwin University		√	
Charles Sturt University		√	√ (acting/interim)
Curtin University		√	√ (acting/interim)
Federation University		√	
Southern Cross University		√	√
Swinburne	√		
University of Adelaide		√	√(acting/interim)*
University of Canberra		√	
University of Queensland	√		
Sunshine Coast	√		
University of Sydney		√	√
UWA		√	
University of Wollongong	√		
Victoria University		√	
TOTALS	4 (27%)	11 (73%)	6 (55% of 11)

Source: Australian university websites, January 2021.

*Update February, 2021: A male was announced as the successful candidate as the next vice-chancellor and will replace the male interim/acting.

Factoring in your invisibility as a woman

Remember my example in Chapter Two of me not being on the decision-makers' radar when they were considering a rare executive leadership acting position? I thought my profile was strong with the decision-makers, but I was wrong. I didn't factor in my invisibility as a woman. The potential to access all opportunities is enhanced by a high or strong profile. Opportunities to join a successful research group, gain greater teaching leadership experience, or oversee the work of others in some way are often *ad hoc*, like in my example. Having a strong profile will increase your chances that the decision-makers will think of you when opportunities arise. Finally, to achieve a strong

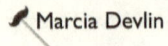
Marcia Devlin

research performance, you will need to have your work 'out there' – I'll talk about this in more detail below.

In essence, there are two aspects to creating and raising your profile. The first is to develop and present your profile and the second is to use your profile to engage with others.

Building a profile

There are a number of essential components of building a profile. These are outlined below. Don't miss any of them.

A **digital profile** is increasingly necessary, and most academics have these on the university's internal websites, though professional women less often. These internal profiles are usually a short summary of your knowledge, skills and experience – sometimes with segments focused on research funds, publications and teaching expertise/commitments. Your background experience can be added, including roles you have held previously, details of your professional association memberships, affiliations and so on. These are a great start.

Evidence of the esteem in which you are held by others is essential to breaking into the boys' club of the professoriate. For example, you need to include any invitational or honorary positions you hold or have held, invitations to present your work or to join a research team that you have received from other universities or from industry or professional bodies and so on. The focus is on facts and on the positive. For example, facts such as, 'I have applied for many jobs I haven't even been shortlisted for' and, 'I have had countless papers rejected from journals' do not appear in any of my public profiles, even though they are true. Your profile should be centred around your primary professional purpose and goals, which I'll talk more about in the next section.

The language you use in your digital profile is important. Describing my contribution to a research team, I could say, 'I contributed to a research project' or, 'I played a leading role in a federally-funded research project focused on [insert primary professional purpose]. This ground-breaking research led to [insert impacts].' Both are true, but the latter version better projects the professional messages about myself I want to emphasise.

Have a professional standard photo as part of your digital profile. I'm sometimes surprised that people choose 'social' photos for their professional profile, often taken while out with friends and enjoying a drink. A picture paints a thousand words and you probably don't want those words about you to be, 'She enjoys a glass of wine or three.' This may well be true (and who doesn't), but it's not the professional image that will help you advance. It is worth investing in professional photos for your profile.

Professional photos are necessary when you apply for awards. I recommend **applying for awards**. Not only will applying hone your profile writing skills – a positive end in itself – but winning an award will raise your profile. Win-win. (See what I did there?)

What if people think I'm up myself?

Like many women I have worked with, you might feel uncomfortable about the idea of having a high profile. You might be thinking of examples of women who have high profiles who you believe are conceited or – to use the Australian vernacular – 'up themselves'. You might find flagrant self-promotion distasteful. You might be tempted to stick to your belief that your achievements will speak for themselves and your good work will be noticed and rewarded. A lot of women at Levels A and B think this way.

Engaging with others

The second part of raising your profile is engagement. To create, maintain and grow your profile, you will need to engage with others. Women are talented at connecting and engaging with others, so here's an advantage we can leverage. Connection and engagement is normally done primarily in person and digitally as a backup (when we're not in a global pandemic). One of the benefits of the pandemic, and of meetings and events having moved online, is that we have been forced to do things differently. This has expanded our minds and skillsets. We have all learnt to engage with others via various digital means. The skills you have learnt and the confidence you have gained through becoming familiar with digital platforms can serve you well in terms of engagement and your profile. Colleagues across the world are now more open to digital connection than in the past. Many opportunities will continue to have a digital access option, even as we move into the new post-COVID-19 normal. Embrace this change. Engaging this way saves time and energy – and you have limited supplies of both.

With all of this in mind, consider the following suggestions:
- Make sure your internal university profile is high quality, up to date and accessible to the outside world.
- When someone in your discipline/department/institution/the sector achieves a milestone or wins an award and puts the details online, congratulate them and add a short complimentary comment. This small action has been the start of many wonderful connections and relationships for me.

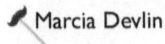

- If you're not already doing so, engaging with social media can bring new connections and opportunities. Watch for a while, take notes and then focus time and effort on creating the profile that will serve your goals best.

Your media profile

Media training offered by your university, including how to write media-friendly – rather than academic – articles, is worth the investment of your time and effort. I had a commissioned column in a major newspaper for 13 years and can attest to the fact that media reach can significantly improve your impact and profile. Let your university's media unit know you are available for interview comments for newspapers, digital outlets, radio and television in areas of your expertise. Do the training they offer. Commenting on and writing digital media articles on platforms like The Conversation, LinkedIn and others will enhance your profile. Ask your university media office for help.

Other ways to raise your profile

As well as having a digital profile and using it to engage with others, there are other ways to raise your profile. To be seen, put yourself forward for opportunities – even if you are unsuccessful. Recently, I applied for a board role. I have significant relevant experience and am a qualified and experienced company director. I rang the board chair before I put in an application and talked to him about the industry, the specific organisation and its context, and briefly about my background and experience. With his encouragement, I applied. I was shortlisted for an interview. I prepared carefully, including speaking to colleagues in the industry and preparing a briefing on each member of the panel. The interview appeared to go well. The process unwound over a three-month period, at the end of which I was quite invested in winning this role. My application was not successful.

While I was nursing my disappointment, a member of the selection panel rang me and explained that she had been asked for recommendations of suitable candidates for a board she had sat on previously. She asked if I would be interested in her putting my name forward. I agreed, and at the time of drafting this chapter, the chair of the second board called and arranged a panel interview for me for the unadvertised vacancy. Now, a few weeks later, while I am editing the chapter, the chair called today to offer me the role. Smiley face.

Getting on decision-makers' radars

You must get on the radar of the decision-makers if you want to advance. Some people call this 'managing up'. It's never too late to start doing this. Busy decision-makers need highly intelligent, competent, energetic people who can help them meet their competing needs and agendas. In other words, they need you.

Some of the strategies I have successfully used include:
- Sending a pithy summary of the main takeaway messages from a meeting/seminar/conference to my boss and/or other senior folk for their interest.
- Sending a copy of an article or report I had written to someone more senior whom I admired, and on whose radar I would like to appear. Senior colleagues are busy people so be careful not to expect anything from them. I have had long-term mentors come from actions like this earlier in my career.
- Ensuring my work is acknowledged as my work by, for example, including my name as the author in the header or footer of the documents I have prepared.
- Ensuring I am thoroughly prepared for, and engaged in, every committee meeting I attend, am seated in the line of sight of the chair, and I am making sensible and useful comments and contributions.
- Offering senior colleagues help with any interesting or challenging projects or initiatives they may be planning (keeping my boss in the loop too).
- Giving senior people compliments.

The power of compliments

After eight years as a university senior executive, I can tell you that there are few compliments flowing up that way. Grumblings, yes. Gripes, yes. Complaints, yes. Insults, yes. Threats (at times), yes. Requests for more money, almost daily. Compliments? Not often. Yet compliments are extremely powerful. So powerful, in fact, that it's a wonder they haven't been bottled and sold.

Think about how you feel when someone says something positive about your work or you. While you might feel a bit uncomfortable (and if so, please do try to get over that ASAP), is there anything more warming or motivating than being told that you are valued? Senior decision-makers are human too. We have feelings – when we are not busy being Evil Overlords/Overladies bent on destroying your life, of course.

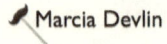

If you decide to give complimenting a go, be genuine in both your intent and the content of your positive feedback – senior people can spot a phoney and an attempted manipulation as well as anyone. But I'll let you in on a secret. If you give a senior person a compliment, you are in a rare minority and you will stand out – in a good way. Add to your compliment a request to consider you for any opportunity coming up and you have just put yourself on a decision-maker's radar.

> *As an academic, you have a responsibility to have a high profile.*

On the other hand, the vast majority of female professors I know are skilled at boasting without appearing to be boasting – including me. I blow my own trumpet while pretending I don't even own a trumpet. I'm good at this. If I wasn't good at this, I wouldn't have made it to professor, senior vice-president or senior deputy vice-chancellor – and I wouldn't be writing this book. I would not have been in a position to help hundreds of women advance in universities, which is my primary professional purpose. I would not have had the breadth of impact in my fields of research. I would not have had my work cited over 4,000 times to date. (Do I sound a bit boastful here? Would I sound as boastful if I were a man? Should I stick on my false moustache before I continue?)

Where was I? Oh, yes, being up myself. As an academic, you have a responsibility to have a high profile. Hear me out. For example, if you are undertaking research, you have a responsibility to share the learnings from that research in appropriate forums and with as many people as possible – people who will benefit from knowing about what you have created or discovered. If you are reluctant, start with a scholarly site such as ResearchGate and observe how it works. There's a bit of trumpeting going on. But there is also a gateway to interesting work and like-minded colleagues. Of course, you might already be on here and other sites, and have a profile. *Up the ante.* You think you have a profile but remember, as a woman, you are actually somewhat invisible, and people assume you're only interested in the cakes, carpets, curtains and colours. Assume all you've done on your profile is not enough and do some more.

That said, raising and maintaining your public profile is a careful balancing act – it's not a matter of bombarding every platform and contact with constant 24/7 updates about what a champ you are. Think of someone you know who is always on LinkedIn or Twitter, posting his thought bubbles about whatever. Super annoying. You will need to be nuanced – something at which women also excel. Include a profile-raising strand in your 10, 5, 2 and 1 year plans. Figure out a goal – for example, 'Raise my ResearchGate score' – then work out what actions you will take to achieve this goal.

You might feel shy about blowing your own trumpet. Look at the profile of some senior women you admire. How do they create and maintain their profile? What would you be comfortable emulating? (Emulating is a fancy word for 'copying'. I've copied lots of people's profiles. They don't know. Or if they do, they have been too polite to say so. Besides, copying is the best form of flattery.) You might remember the point I made in Chapter Two about being expected to show humility and worry that you might appear to be boastful or up yourself. I understand your concern. It's a balancing act being a successful woman in academia. Try softly trumpeting – at least a little bit. *Toot-toot-toot-toot.* Don't lie in your profile but do put your best foot forward. Why would you do anything else? One or two people might think you are up yourself – who cares? They're probably jealous of your fabulous, growing profile and the amazing professional photo you are using. They'll probably start copying you before long.

You might also be concerned about the apparent incongruence between raising your profile and meeting your gendered expectations. It took me years to feel comfortable writing boastful bios for speaking gigs. (You write these yourself, the host reads them out and then you get up and say, with your head slightly bowed like Princess Diana, 'Thank you so much for that very kind introduction' *that you actually wrote to make yourself sound fabulous.* It's a bit of a game.) One trick I've learnt to manage the humility/gravitas conundrum is to focus your profile on your work and its outcomes and impact– rather than on you, *per se.*

But if you insist on being safe and continuing to be a good girl, all you need to do is say yes to everything, do all of the housework at home and at work, and keep a low profile. Voilá, you're a Level A forever. But I don't think that's what you want. You are reading this book because you are open to doing at least some of what is needed to advance – and if you want to advance, you need to raise your profile. Having a profile counts. What are you going to do first? When? Put it in your calendar so you don't forget.

Focus on what counts for promotion

Because it is so complex, this section focuses primarily on the academic promotion route in detail. If you're a professional woman, start skim-reading from here – but tune back in at the heading 'Watch out for traps'. Then return to skim-reading at the heading 'Focus on research' but please make sure you tune in again at the heading 'Making time to write and publish (and other important things)' – this contains good general time-saving/efficiency and self-care advice). Then skim-read the teaching section and tune back in for the rest of the chapter at 'Lead whenever possible'.

If you want to be in the professoriate, you will need to move up the academic levels from A toward E or secure increasingly higher-level professional roles. There are at least two ways to get further up the hierarchy: Apply elsewhere or get promoted in your current institution.

Applying for a higher-level role elsewhere

One way to advance is to apply for a higher-level role at another university. I've done this successfully, as have many women I know. There are pros and cons to leaving one institution for another, but often your perceived value is higher elsewhere than it is where you currently work. Leverage that perceived value. If your application elsewhere is successful, you can either accept the higher-level role or ask your current university to consider matching the offer so that you can stay. Many men do this – not so many women.

I became a professor in 2008, when there were just over 2,500 women working full-time in the professoriate in Australia. I had no idea I was part of such a tiny cohort at the time. But I did know that, prior to moving institutions to take up a chair position, I had little chance of becoming a professor where I was. There were multiple male professors in my department but no females above Level C. As I departed the university I had been at (on and off) for five years, my (male) line manager commented to a colleague that the university I was going to was 'not a real university' (meaning it was not an elite university), and that therefore I 'wouldn't be a real professor'. I laughed at his stupidity, took up the chair, accepted a significant pay rise and did career-defining work at the new institution.

A friend recently left a university where she had been an associate professor and head of a large school for many years. She applied for promotion to professor at her university – and failed. Despite knocking her application back, the (female) dean asked my friend to continue being the head of school because she was *so good at it*. It wouldn't help her get promoted, necessarily, the dean explained, but it was really so *very helpful* to the university. I'm pleased to report that my friend is now a professor (and dean!) at another university.

Take a strategic approach to being promoted

The second way to advance is to either up the academic scales by applying for promotion within your institution or seeking a higher-level professional role within your institution.

Achieving academic promotion in higher education can appear to be fairly straightforward. Universities have promotion policies that set out the criteria for successful progression through the alphabetic levels – which generally refer to the three aspects of academic work: teaching, research, and administration/service/leadership. There are often variations to accommodate research-focused and teaching-focused appointments, and sometimes other variations. However, despite these variations, there is often still an unspoken privileging of research performance.

> *You'll need to plan ahead and think carefully about how to put forward a gold standard application – and when to do so.*

The rules are supposedly the same for men and women. But men get promoted more often than women – because of sexism, as I outlined in Chapter Two. Some of the factors I discuss in Chapter Two play out during promotion application processes. Having sat on and chaired many promotion committees, I have seen that sexism and unconscious bias are often subtly at play in promotion panels' decision-making. I have also observed a clear privileging of research performance over performance in other areas. Since women say yes to so many requests that don't help them advance, and get stuck doing the housework at home and at work, they don't have the time, energy or opportunity to privilege research the way many men do. I'll talk about research in more detail below.

While universities continue to work on that problem, you need to take a strategic approach to getting promoted. You'll need to plan ahead and think carefully about how to put forward a gold standard application – and when to do so. The advice on strategic preparation for a successful promotion application is roughly the same for men and women, but there are nuances for women that I will discuss below as I outline the standard advice on maximising your chances of being promoted.

And although now a little dated in some ways, I recommend Royce Sadler's classic book, *Managing your Academic Career: Strategies for Success*[29] as a good general source of advice.

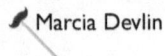
Marcia Devlin

Choose your timing carefully

Plan for a promotion application as early as possible. A young female colleague recently promoted to Level B told me that, on hearing the good news about her successful application, she had *immediately* started her evidence file for Level C. I feel confident about her chances of beating the odds.

Make the decision about whether or not to apply in a particular year carefully – taking your context, definition of success, plan and goals into account. For example, I didn't apply for promotion (or plan to move institutions) in a year when Finn or Aengus were in a transition year in their education. I knew that they both needed additional time and energy from me that year, and that it would be better to wait and build the evidence base for a stronger promotion application a year or two later.

Putting together an outstanding application takes significant time and energy, which can be wasted if the timing is not right for you. Writing an application is time and energy taken away from other activities such as research and writing that might be necessary to 'tick all the boxes' to ensure the strongest application possible. You also need to be aware of technical barriers to the timing of a promotion, such as a requirement that you must be at the top of your current level to be eligible. Also be aware of re-application rules – such as a two year moratorium after an unsuccessful application.

A word of warning: The decision about when to apply is yours. A colleague who was recently (and deservedly) promoted to associate professor told me a story that I have heard in many forms previously. As she began to consider applying for promotion, she mentioned to a junior male colleague that she was thinking of applying. He immediately told her confidently, 'You're not ready.' He was a lecturer and junior to my then senior lecturer colleague, but he felt fully equipped to assess and pass comments on her fitness for application from senior lecturer to associate professor. The same woman told me that as she built her profile and this started to bear fruit for her, a male professor in her research group pulled her up. He complained to her that because she was doing so well and had a rising profile, he 'felt invisible' (welcome to our world, honey). He suggested that my colleague 'do a better job' of promoting *him*. You can't make this stuff up.

I often see male supervisors telling strong female candidates they are 'not ready' for promotion and/or that they 'need more time' at their current level. Personal readiness (whatever that means and however that is measured) and 'time spent' are not formal criteria for promotion in any university in which I have worked or have consulted. But these criteria exist in the ether around decision-makers. Using these unofficial criteria is a subtle way of holding back talented women who are set to beat the odds. Sometimes, in promotion panel meetings, I wonder if comments from males like, 'She's not ready,' or, 'She's only been a [insert level] for [insert amount of time],' is code for '*I'm* not ready to see her advance or succeed.'

Whether you are ready to apply for promotion is a judgement call, but it is your call. You can seek input on your decision from trusted advisers and colleagues, but perhaps give the guy who is unsettled by your outstanding performance a wide berth.

Watch out for traps

Many women fall into 'traps' in academia that limit their advancement. As I mentioned in Chapter Three, women are often people pleasers. My observations over three decades in universities tell me that women in academia often try to help and please others, and these desires can lead to being trapped at lower levels. For example, as I said in Chapter Three, if you are an academic at Level A, B or even C, you need to be careful about accepting excessive teaching and/or low-level but time-consuming administrative responsibilities. While they may be appropriate for a time, the 'trap' is that you end up accepting them for too long. Many women tell me that had they understood better how this creates obstacles to academic promotion, they would have started renegotiating excessive teaching and administrative duties earlier – and insisted on doing only their fair share.

Heavy teaching workloads are a common trap for academic women. Being excellent – even exceptional – at teaching will not, on its own, lead to promotion, even if you have a teaching-focused position. If you are being subjected to unfair practices in the area of teaching allocations, you have the right to ask for your workload to be reviewed. You will also need to be aware that this may lead to disapproval (you're not being a good girl if you ask for this sort of thing), but it is your right. These reviews are often helpful in uncovering inequities and can be used as the basis for renegotiating.

For professional women – watch out for large quantities of repetitive, mind-numbingly boring work that is repeated on a cyclical basis. Consider introducing some form of automation for this work, or creating a more efficient work flow or task sharing. Not only will these options relieve you of the burden of this sort of work, but creating and implementing these solutions can be added to your CV as evidence of your ability to innovate.

Being micromanaged is another trap. Restrictive management practices where you are not allowed to develop, take risks, experiment and innovate pose an obstacle to promotion. You will find it difficult to show in a promotion

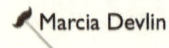

application that you have added value beyond 'just doing your job'. Be aware and try to negotiate these issues early with your line manager. Seek advice and help early from approachable senior colleagues, human resources or your union.

A particular trap for many women is one that I call 'the deputy trap'. A woman takes a job as a deputy of some kind; for example, deputy coordinator, deputy head, deputy director, deputy (or associate) dean or deputy vice-chancellor. These roles appear to be a great opportunity – and, in many ways, they are. Women excel at these roles. They are all about proactive and pre-emptive organising, smoothing and fixing. Much of the work is invisible. It is about anticipating where trouble might lurk and neutralising it before it takes form, predicting risk and turning it into opportunity, and supporting – never outshining – the boss. All from the back room. These roles, done well, are extremely challenging and can also be dangerous. Sold to women as a leadership opportunity, they do provide useful exposure to aspects of leadership, as well as valuable experience. But, ironically, they can also hold you back from leading and being seen to lead, and, therefore, ironically, from other leadership opportunities.

I was once asked – as a lecturer (Level B) – to 'keep an eye on' 10 casual staff. Ten. This meant: recruit; train; find desks and computers for; support; supervise; replace when ill; arrange payment of; answer emails from; resolve conflicts between; and manage all day-to-day issues for 10 people. Ten. This work took me up to 15 hours a week. I was given no workload allocation for this supervisory work because I was just keeping an eye on them, no big deal. And the 'opportunity' provided nothing formal to put on my CV because these staff officially reported to my boss, for whom I was an informal deputy.

It is hard to show you can lead when your job is – literally – to help ensure someone else is a brilliant leader and to keep your part in this secret. If you're really good at being a deputy, your boss won't even notice what or how much you do, so he's probably not going to be much use to your ambitions to lead. I don't have a simple answer to the deputy trap. I suffered it myself a number of times. Be aware of it, and if you figure out how to navigate it better than I did, please let me know.

Methodically gather and document your evidence

Your academic promotion application or application for a higher-level professional role requires robust evidence to back assertions and claims you make. You will need to gather all the evidence you have of your performance that is relevant to the type of appointment you have and to the level at which you are seeking promotion. Many women are not good at doing this and instead just focus on 'getting the job done'. I strongly recommend collecting, on an ongoing basis, anything that you can add to your professional portfolio that provides evidence of the quality of the work you are doing. This is so important that I have a framework for it — I call it 'Record, Reflect, Request, Report' or 'the 4Rs' for short.

Record

Record your achievements regularly in whatever way works for you. Every Friday afternoon, I open my computer and type into an achievements file what I have done and achieved that week. I use dot points and it takes just a few minutes. I have a second file in which I collate unsolicited, positive, work-related emails or other messages from colleagues or students that I get sent from time to time. I also update my CV every time I have another publication or invited address, or any dot point of some kind to add. The records are handy when I am looking for evidence of things I have done to address promotion or selection criteria. You must have impact and have evidence of that impact. This is something you need to tease out from the tasks or roles you have undertaken. You acted in a senior role for a few months? Great, put that down, but what were the impacts of you doing so? What value did you add and what is the evidence of that? Spell this out in detail as well.

Rather than just getting on with doing everything and, by omission, minimising your contributions, you instead detail them and, thereby, maximise.

Generally speaking, women aren't as good at articulating the details of what they have contributed and value-added as men. We minimise. We downplay our achievements and their impacts. This is to help us meet the gendered expectations of being modest. Men don't do this — they maximise. Remember the guy who put in his promotion application that his research performance had been negatively affected because *his wife* had had a baby? His description of the contribution he made in the home and the negative impact on his productivity was detailed and therefore somewhat compelling and convincing. Imagine that — rather than just getting on with doing everything and, by omission, minimising your contributions, you instead detailed them and, thereby, maximised? If you put in a case for equity (also known as a case for assessment of 'performance relative to opportunity') as part of your academic promotion application, channel this guy. Put on your false moustache if it helps (and possibly a false beard as well).

Your record of achievements will help you maximise. I also visit the files and collections I keep if I'm having a bad day or hard time. They remind me of the positive impacts I am having and have had – and that makes me feel better. Especially the unsolicited emails. By the way, if you think a woman you know is fabulous at her job or an aspect of her job, take a small break from reading this book to write her an email and tell her how fabulous she is and why. She'll appreciate and benefit from it, and she can add it to her file. And who knows? She might do the same for you.

Reflect

Review and reflect on your records periodically. As well as improving your mood (as visiting mine does for me), reflecting on your records can provide insight into what you are doing well and about the areas in which you need to improve and grow. One female colleague was knocked back in her application for promotion to professor, partly because she failed to maximise. She had a stunning record – acting dean in a challenging environment for numerous and substantive periods of time, including between the appointments of (male) deans and through two periods of tumultuous institutional change. Her substantive deputy dean position (which she undertook concurrently while being acting dean) had responsibilities that covered all aspects of faculty strategy and operations*.

But on reflection, she merely mentioned these significant roles in her application and provided no detail about her outstanding leadership impact. On reviewing her unsuccessful application at her request, I asked her why she had not detailed the impact she had made, and she said, 'I thought being acting dean for so many months and deputy dean for years would speak for itself.' As much as promotion panels desperately want to help candidates, they cannot assume what is not in the application. Don't be a minimiser. Be a maximiser. Put on that false moustache if it might help you to think differently.

For academic promotion, you may wish to take reflection a step further. You might consider conducting an audit of your performance in all three areas specified in your university's promotion policy. Note the areas or criteria where you need more evidence. Amend your personal strategic plans to include appropriate development activities and ways to generate evidence of impact. For professional promotion, you might like to collect and review a few position descriptions of higher-level roles from positions advertised at

---

* After hearing about her deputy duties, I asked her what the dean spent his time doing. She said, 'I don't know. He goes to lunch a lot.' I thought to myself, 'I'll bet he does with a stellar deputy like this.'

your university and other universities. What sorts of experience, capabilities and skills do these higher-level positions call for? Amend your personal strategic plans to include appropriate development activities and ways to gain the necessary exposure to develop into the higher-level roles.

Request

Request feedback on your work, performance, leadership, collegiality – anything on which you think it might be helpful to have the views of others. These can help you reflect and validate – and, where necessary, improve. This might sound cheeky (it is perfectly legal and ethical), but ask for endorsements from colleagues in areas in which you excel. For example, you can ask trusted colleagues to write down the impacts you or your work have had on them, their work, students or whatever is relevant, and send it to you in an email. You can ask for recommendations on LinkedIn. Don't be afraid to offer to draft these recommendations or endorsements for busy colleagues. And then return the favour.

Report

'Report' refers to reporting your achievements and esteem in annual performance appraisals, in job applications, on your profile(s), in promotion applications, or wherever useful. Remember to maximise, maximise, maximise. Put on your false moustache if necessary. You can also report on your reflections and actions that you have taken to address areas in need of improvement. This plays well with academic promotion applications in particular.

Later in the book I talk about using the 4Rs when things go wrong. But for now, consider using the 4R system to help you advance.

Ask for help

Applying for promotion is not a solitary activity. You do not have to do it alone. Asking for help is sensible. In the case of promotion, asking for help might be something that gives us an edge in beating the odds. Ever been in a car with a man who is lost? Did you notice that he will drive for hours (or even days or, quite possibly, weeks) in the wrong direction rather than stop and ask for help? Yep. Here's something that might be an advantage for us women – we have no qualms about asking for help. In addition, no-one is going to get upset with us asking for help because it fits in with sexist notions that we are not quite as fabulous and knowledgeable as men. Ask for all the help you can get, and then some.

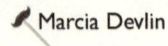
Marcia Devlin

Most universities offer academic promotion information sessions specifically for women. Go to these. Listen. Ask questions. Follow the advice given. Senior staff within your discipline may also be willing to advise or mentor you and/or to help you to navigate applying for promotion. A generous senior colleague may offer to read and comment on your application. But rather than search for 'the one' who can help you, find several colleagues who have been through the promotions process in your university and ask them all for help. Be aware that senior women are often approached by junior women for help with promotion applications. Sometimes the senior women have to say no. Be prepared for this (and understand that saying no is part of the reason she got to, and stays at, a senior level and remains sane). Don't let this put you off – you can find help from others. Be inspired by her ability to say no.

Reading successful academic applications can be helpful in demystifying the process of applying. See if there are any generous colleagues inside or outside your area and institution who may be willing to share their successful applications with you. Devour them (the successful applications – not your colleagues).

If you are a professional woman, look for leadership development programs inside and outside your university and enrol in these – they will help you develop knowledge and skills and, by doing them, you will be demonstrating drive and initiative.

Whether you are an academic or professional woman, start letting the relevant people know that you are thinking about promotion, while being mindful of implicit expectations, unconscious bias and the negative way in which an ambitious woman can be viewed. Make an appointment with your current line manager/head of department and/or dean (after getting advice from senior colleagues about the politics of who you approach and in what order). Take along your CV, using your senior colleagues' as a model, and the clear and supported argument you have prepared about why giving you promotion would be beneficial to the discipline/department/faculty/institution/universe. If this person says, 'You're not ready,' or, 'You've only been at level X for [insert amount of time],' do the following:

1. Choose your attitude carefully (see Chapter Three).
2. Ask a 'more details please' question. For example, 'What do you mean by "not ready" exactly?' or, 'Why is the fact that I've been at [insert level] for [insert amount of time] relevant to whether or not I apply for promotion/a higher-level role?'
3. Listen carefully to their response and note down what they say.

4. Ask another question, this time focused on solutions. For example, 'What would you need to see that would show you that I am "ready"?' or, 'What amount of time do you believe I need to be at level X and why?'
5. Listen carefully to their response and note down what they say.
6. Summarise what they have said and ask them if that is a fair summary.
7. Listen carefully to their response and note down what they say.
8. Thank them for their time and insights.

Then use the 4R framework to consider what you have heard and learnt in this meeting.

If you have previously applied for promotion or a higher-level role and not succeeded, ask for a meeting with the chair of the promotion or recruitment and selection committee. Use a version of the process above. Ask which aspects of your performance and/or the application need improvement, and for frank feedback on how you can improve your chances of success next time. Then use the 4R framework again.

Focus on research

Research counts. Some might argue it counts too much. If you want to get promoted in most universities, you need to focus on research or its equivalent, such as scholarship for teaching-focused positions and creative works in fields like art and performance. The aspects of traditional research that count include grants/funding, publications, citations and impact, and the discipline-specific variations of these. There are different emphases and rules around which of these are more or less important, depending on your discipline, institutional promotion policy and other norms. This book does not detail how to become a brilliant researcher – this is a nuanced and discipline-specific endeavour. Asking for help will be useful in understanding what counts in your unique situation.

One of the best ways to build your research is to join an active research team. This is easy for me to say but can be a bit tricky to do. You can't just waltz up to a successful team and say, 'Hey, can I join in?' However, most women are good at offering to help others and this can work to your advantage. Approach the research group or team leader. If you have followed my earlier advice about raising your profile, s/he might even have heard of you. Offer to undertake research-related tasks such as:

- contributing to the literature review;
- collating questionnaire responses;
- proofreading or copyediting draft papers;

- doing administrative work related to the research (not for too long); and
- if you have the skills and experience, interviewing participants or facilitating focus group interviews.

I got my start in research by doing many of the things on this list.

This list is not exhaustive and you will be able to think of additional suggestions relevant to your discipline area. The payoff will come from the experience, learning, collaborative relationships, getting on the radar of researchers who are ahead of you, and perhaps even an invitation to join a later grant bid. You will need to be aware of the potential trap (another one!) of becoming an ongoing, unpaid research assistant, but I'm confident you will know when and how to avoid that. Whatever it is, make sure you document your contributions and the joint outcomes from the research as evidence you can use for promotion applications.

> *You need to be strategic about ensuring the dollars are evident in your application.*

Grants and funding

To advance, you will need to win grants and otherwise secure funding. This is difficult and is becoming more so. Women find it harder than men. There are depressing analyses that show the percentage of Australian Research Council funds that go to men versus women but I'm not going to report them here – I'm trying to inspire and motivate you rather than depress you further. You need to be strategic about ensuring the dollars are evident in your application. Every dollar counts, and from little things big things grow – so every opportunity to win funds or be on a team that wins funds is a valuable one. Ask at the university research office about small grants available to newer researchers. Invest time in seminars that provide advice to potential applicants on how to write successful grant applications. I self-funded some of my early research activity to get runs on the board, which helped win external funds later. I don't necessarily recommend this, but it is an option.

I know universities *should* provide funding to get us started in research, and that men and women *should* win funds at similar rates. But in Chapter Three I told you that – although I agree with many 'shoulds' – the problem is that many things that 'should' happen haven't happened and/or aren't happening in useful ways for women. Providing adequate funding for research can go in this basket. In the meantime, you need to decide what you are going to do. Get an attitude and get to work. Grants and funding count.

Publications and citations

The general advice around publications is the same for men and women — publish in high-ranking journals and get cited a lot. I'm not able to go into a lot of detail about how to do that here. Generally, publishing is harder for women — as is getting cited — because women are too busy meeting good girl expectations, saying yes to requests and doing all the housework instead of writing papers and doing the promotion work necessary to get their work in front of others. In order to be successful in building publications and citations, you will need to carve out time and protect it from other demands. Ask senior colleagues about how they have done this — there are many 'tricks' to achieving writing and publication goals. These include:

- having things set up so you can easily write for 20 minutes every day or twice a day;
- getting up early in the morning to write;
- taking a block of time out each fortnight to focus on writing;
- setting and meeting deadlines with a writing 'buddy'; and
- other tricks that your senior colleagues are likely to be happy to share with you.

Make time to write and publish (and do other important things)

I have about 320 publications. These include refereed and research outputs, and media and popular publications. I write a lot. I'll share some of my time tricks below. I was drawn to an article by Travis Bradberry published on LinkedIn in 2016, called 'Critical things ridiculously successful people do every day'[30]. The title made me laugh out loud but, after reading it, I stopped laughing and adopted most of the pieces of advice in the article that weren't already part of my practice. The advice came from interviews of more than 200 ultra-successful people who were asked, 'What is your number one secret to productivity?' My version of how to be productive — particularly in writing and publishing — draws heavily on this article as well as on a presentation by a woman called Denni Francisco on being your own CEO (Chief Energy Officer)[31].

1. Do the most important things first each day. Before I adopted this advice, I used to 'get ready' before I started 'real work'. Shower, breakfast, chatting to family, grooming, patting the cat, cleaning out the toaster crumb tray, putting a load of clothes on to wash, cleaning the fluff out of the dryer filter (someone has to do this), checking social media, watering my plants, checking emails and so on. Today I got out of bed, ate toast and drank tea while the computer fired up, and then sat down to write this chapter. I've learned to do the things that count first. (I will shower later, by the way.)

2. Focus on minutes, not hours. Many women I know wait for an hour (or a few hours in a row) uninterrupted before undertaking the most important work. These long blocks rarely, if ever, come between meeting housework and other womanly expectations. For me, and for women I've coached, 20 minutes is plenty of time to get something done. There are three 20-minute slots in an hour – that's three things done and off the list. Try it.
3. Put all the tasks on your 'to do' list into your calendar. Then do the tasks at the allocated time. That's it. If they don't fit in the 168 hours in the week – there's a hint for you – what are you going to say no to or start doing so badly you stop being asked to do it?
4. Manage your meetings tightly – only attend the ones you absolutely have to attend, and if you're chairing, finish on time or early.
5. Process emails only a few times a day. Turn email off in between. Try it. Really, try this one.
6. Have regular breaks from social media. I know I have encouraged you to get on the socials but recently I watched the disturbing Netflix documentary *The Social Dilemma*. Now I'm trying to have 24–36 hours off socials each week. My mental health has improved and I'm getting more done.
7. Touch things only once. For example, when you open an email, assess it and respond, categorise, file or delete it immediately.
8. Become the CEO of your life – the Chief Energy Officer. Practise self-care through diet, exercise, sleep, rest and work practices that make you the healthiest and most energetic you can possibly be.
9. Anticipate your future self-sabotage and pre-emptively thwart yourself. I love this one. For example, I used to often not exercise and find wonderful excuses. Now I anticipate my future self and:
    a. schedule the exercise in my diary, including travel time;
    b. lay out the clothes, swipe cards and/or equipment I'll need the night before;
    c. set an exercise alarm; and
    d. write myself a motivating note, just in case.

I find my past self very annoying in the future, but it works. Most of the time.

You might wonder about numbers eight and nine, which are not directly to do with work productivity. They are included because they underpin productivity. We are not machines, so we need to look after our whole selves. Women find this hard – but you are worth it, as we'll discuss in the next chapter.

So now you are publishing like mad and need to get cited. As one key plank of your citation strategy, you need to have a high profile. Re-read that section and get to work.

Be prepared to do most of it in your own time

Having sufficient time for research is an issue for most academics. My friend and colleague Matt Brett recently said that being an academic gives you great freedom – you work 70 hours a week and you can freely choose how to use those 70 hours. Cue some 'shoulds'; for example, governments should fund universities better, and then university Evil Overlords/Overladies (also known as managers) should give academics more reasonable workloads. In the meantime, it might be up to each of us to do what we can within the realities of modern university life. Many academics find that, even when there is officially an allocation of time in your workload for research, it is hard to stop other duties spilling into your research time. You will need to be prepared to do at least some research in your own time. Given the gendered expectations of you, and all the yeses you are uttering, and the amount of housework you have, this will be particularly hard for you. Unless you say no more often and stop trying to be 'The Perfect Housewife'.

Over my career, I did much of my research activity – particularly writing – in the evenings and on weekends when my children were being looked after by their father or grandparents, or were occupied or asleep. I did not do as much socialising as my non-academic friends. I did not have any hobbies for 20 years. I lived by a timetable that marked out each minute of the day – it was military-like in its precision. I definitely did not do housework when I could be doing research work (I do housework when I am too tired to do anything else, need time out to think, need a workout, or it otherwise suits me). One female professor I know deliberately does not have a television in her house. She says she saves a lot of time that others waste watching television and uses that time to progress her research. She is internationally renowned and her publication list is over 100 pages long. Over 100 pages! She is also an attentive and present mother of two young children. And great company. If you have been resisting the idea of saying no and being bad at housework, you might now be coming around to why I recommend these actions so strongly. You need to be ruthless about protecting time for research.

Be clever with teaching

This section is short because if you have a typical academic appointment and want to get promoted, you do need to focus on teaching – but not too much. Compared to research and some forms of leadership service, teaching

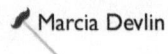
Marcia Devlin

is not as highly valued for promotion. I say this as a teacher, an educator and a fierce advocate for the value of the hard and essential core business work required to facilitate student learning. I also say it as a former member and chair of promotion committees, coach and mentor of scores of female academics and a successful academic. Be clever with teaching – keep it 'doable' as well as high quality.

Make sure your strong performance in teaching is evident in student evaluations. If these evaluations are favourable, you can include them with your application. If they are less than perfect, you can still use them to demonstrate reflection on and improvement in areas of lesser strengths in teaching. Don't forget to contextualise student evaluations. Over many years I've noticed a general trend of more males teaching at postgraduate levels – with students who know how to succeed academically, smaller classes and fewer assignments to mark. I've seen more females teaching at undergraduate levels – with inexperienced tertiary students new to university-level study who need greater amounts of support, with large classes and student numbers, and many more assessments to mark. If you are one of these women, the invisible 'housework' of caring for the needs of many hundreds of new and transitioning students is part of your context and needs to be spelt out. Time to maximise, not minimise.

One woman I mentored told me she had watched how significant retention strategies she had put in place for undergraduate students had led to greater numbers of students being retained and succeeding than was the case before her intervention. Some of these students were so successful, they then went on to become higher degree by research (HDR) students. They were supervised by male colleagues who had less undergraduate teaching and more time for HDRs – and this helped the male colleagues to improve their research records. This woman, denied promotion despite an outstanding record in teaching and student support, learnt to document the initiatives she put in place, collect evidence of their impact and put these details forward in her applications for promotion and for leadership opportunities. She is now an associate professor on her way to professor.

Remember the evidence on gender bias in teaching evaluations I told you about in Chapter Three? The full details are in the References section. Consider including reference to this work in your application as a note for the panel to consider. Choose your attitude carefully.

Use other forms of evidence about the quality of your teaching too. Consider asking an experienced colleague to observe your teaching and/or review your curriculum materials and give you feedback. Document this and any improvements you make following this feedback. Seek and follow advice from your central learning and teaching centre about excellence in learning and teaching. Document your innovations, the ways you have enabled inclusion and your authentic assessments. Maximise. Think about the ways you have contributed to raising the quality of teaching in your unit, course, department, faculty and/or institution – perhaps even more widely. Document this. Don't forget to maximise.

Lead whenever possible

This section is also relatively short. Demonstrating leadership (sometimes also called administration and/or service) will help you advance up the professional staff levels and will help get you promoted as an academic, but not on its own. Consider opportunities for leadership experience carefully.

I took on a new role when my children were in primary school. It was a senior role but without significant people management responsibilities. In essence, I was engaged to create a cross-university research group and ensure we succeeded in meeting the goals of improved grant funding, more high-quality publications, improved teaching quality and improved research and capability development. It was the perfect role for me at the time. Six weeks after I started, the deputy vice-chancellor to whom I reported asked to see me. He told me an opportunity had arisen to lead the large central learning and teaching development support area. It would entail strategic and operational responsibility for improving the quality of learning and teaching in our large university – scores of staff in multiple teams across a number of campuses, who needed to work with hundreds of academics and thousands of students. He told me that I had all the requisite experience and expertise to undertake this role – and he offered it to me.

This was a pivotal moment. There were pros and cons each way if I took the job or passed up the opportunity. But as primary caregiver for two children – with a partner who worked long hours in a non-family-friendly corporate role and travelled a lot, and no other family support nearby – and after discussing and workshopping it with my husband – I declined the offer.

A man was appointed to the role and so began a new relationship navigating our overlapping areas of responsibility. We started off well. He came to dinner in our home, and I worked hard to support and assist him as he settled into his new role. But long story short, things did not go smoothly. Tensions developed and persisted. It was not a happy time. I thought more than once that perhaps I just should have taken the job.

Despite the outcome, and my thoughts at times, declining the offer was one right decision. Taking on the role would have been another right decision. My husband and I could have made it work with some paid help and more use of before- and after-school care programs (which the kids LOVED, by the way, and complained bitterly about not being allowed to go to more often). The leadership development opportunities that taking that role would have provided would have been highly valuable, in retrospect.

But my definition of success at the time included being the best mother I could possibly be, and I judged that a huge leadership role would have precluded that. I wanted to be present for the children. I have to tell you that the children, now young adults, have no memory of me being the primary caregiver for them at all. Not one memory. Except, occasionally, prompted by a photograph and a story from me about the day we did something particularly 'memorable'. They don't remember the playdough I made by hand*. They don't remember the way I set up our house like a play centre when they were small to facilitate their fine and gross motor skill development. Nor the carefully curated fun experiences I created for them at the zoo, park, Scienceworks and the rest to nurture their imagination and cognitive skills. Nor the endless playdates I facilitated to assist their emotional and social development. Nor the countless after-school and holiday activities I researched, selected, vetted and drove them to and from. Nor the fact that I worked part-time for eight years (and stayed at Level B for nearly 13 years) so I could be there and present for them. They remember nothing. None. Of. It. In fact, when my oldest son Finn was about 20, he told a family friend at a party at our house that he and Aengus had 'basically raised ourselves. Mum was so focused on her career.' There are a few lessons in this anecdote – I'll leave it up to you to determine what they might be.

There are many ways to demonstrate leadership or service. For example, you can volunteer for committee service. Not only will this provide brownie points in terms of an academic promotion application, it will also provide you with the opportunity to influence policy and practice, as well as providing valuable knowledge about how the university operates – which can help whether you are an academic or professional staff member. Start off in your department and faculty but also seek university-wide opportunities to broaden your horizons, experience and networks.

There is no simple 'right' answer to developing leadership experiences but if you are offered such experiences, think carefully before you accept

---

* I know. What was I thinking? Don't do this. Let them play with (i.e. eat) commercial playdough – they'll be fine.

them or turn them down. The section below on saying no may be helpful to your decision-making. When it comes to detailing them in your promotion application, focus on your impact and maximise, maximise, maximise.

Choose your referees carefully

You will need referees for a promotion application – and also if you are seeking to move institutions. Choose your referees carefully. I have seen many applications for promotion damned with faint praise from a supposedly trusted referee. Watch out for old fogeys who think you are 'not ready' or that you 'haven't served your time'. Don't be afraid to ask potential referees to focus their reference on particular aspects of your work and to remind them of some of your achievements. I ask everyone who asks me to be a referee to draft the reference for me. I then edit it – adding and subtracting as I see fit. Consider drafting the reference for your referee's consideration. Ensure your referees have a sufficient level of seniority and credibility for the level of role you are applying for.

Adding it all up

Let's recap. To advance in academia as a woman, you need to:
- raise your profile and let the world know about your value;
- take a strategic approach to being promoted and weave it into your broader strategy and plans;
- choose your timing carefully and be on the lookout for traps;
- maximise, maximise, maximise and not minimise your contributions as you gather your evidence (a false moustache may assist);
- ask for help;
- focus on your research;
- be clever with teaching;
- lead where possible; and
- choose your referees carefully.

Got it?

You might feel that this all sounds a bit over the top, and that focusing on yourself like this goes against the grain of the collegiality you value in academia. You might feel you would prefer to enjoy participating in academic and professional life rather than constantly focusing on getting ahead. It is true that strategically and stealthily building a case for promotion – including through self-promotion – over many years can feel 'selfish' and even disingenuous. It might sound exhausting. But without a careful approach, like I have outlined in this chapter, you are destined to remain at the lower levels of academia and the professional hierarchy. If you're OK with that, stop reading and give this book to someone else you think might benefit. But if you think that it's at least a tiny bit unfair that your gender will determine your success, take on board the advice I have offered so far and get to work. The next section will help you as well.

Take action: saying no and being the worst at housework

It is now time to up the ante on protecting your time, energy and goodwill. There's a lot to do to secure advancement in academia and only 24 hours in a day – 168 hours in a week. You do not have time to do more of the things that count for advancement while you keep doing all the things you are currently doing that don't count. I now ask you to make 'no' your favourite word and do the domestic and institutional housework so badly that people start asking if you are OK*.

Make no your favourite word

In the previous chapter, I asked you to start practising saying no. I got the opportunity to say no myself while working on this book – and I took it. I was offered a second term on a board I had served on for three years. The offer letter arrived attached to an email. The offer to renew was almost identical to the previous offer three years earlier except – wait for it – the position changed from being paid to being unpaid. I waited a day (to let my anger subside), selected a calm and determined attitude and wrote back. I thanked the (male) CEO for his email. I said, 'I'm afraid I don't take on pro-bono board work so, regrettably, I will have to decline your offer.' In case he needed to understand further, I added, 'Perhaps we will have the opportunity to do paid work together in the future – I hope so.' Job done.

I have to tell you, I considered saying yes, despite it being a preposterous 'offer'. I might have said yes if I wasn't writing a book that has such a strong argument about the need for women to say no more often and if I wasn't trying to be a role-model to other women. But I confess that I was worried that the CEO might not like it – or me – if I said no. I was worried that not being on this board anymore might look bad for me, especially when I am seeking new board roles. I was worried that I might never be on a board

---

* One appropriate response here is to put on a fake manic grin and say, 'I. Have. Never. Been. Better.' You will soon be left in peace. Especially if you are wearing the false moustache at the same time.

Do More of What Counts – and Less of What Doesn't

again (I can be a catastrophic thinker at times). I re-read what I had written so far in this book about saying no, and took my own advice. I feel so pleased with myself for saying no. But I do understand it is hard.

I had time to think, adopt an attitude and formulate the response I wanted to send. It isn't always like that when you are asked to do something; for example, if you are approached in person or over the phone. If you need to gather your thoughts, you can try saying something like, 'Well, that's an interesting proposal. Let me have a think about it and get back to you.' Or, 'I'll have to check my diary and let you know.' You can then think through whether or not you really want to, or have to, do what you have been asked to do. You also have time to consider the options for the best way to say no, practise saying no, gather the courage to say no, and deliver your brief, firm, polite 'no' message, with determination and confidence.

Be the worst at housework

In Chapter Three, I mentioned that we, as women, are socialised into doing most of the housework – and practice makes us very good at it indeed. I also mentioned that those around us soon learn that if they do chores badly, they will eventually have the chores taken off them – a ruse that we are complicit in. Let me expand on that now.

> *Wives 'gatekeep' certain high standards of housework that partners and children usually struggle or fail to meet.*

Author Susan Maushart wrote a cracker of a book called *Wifework*[32]. In it, among other things, she points out that 50 percent of marriages end in divorce – and that women are responsible for initiating three-quarters of them. That's certainly another option to saying no to housework. Maushart also points out that wives 'gatekeep' certain high standards of housework that partners and children usually struggle or fail to meet. Reading this in her book stunned me.

I realised that I was a gatekeeper of the standards of laundry folding, and my standards were *very* high (like in a high-end shop where there is only one of each 'piece' on display, and each is like an artwork). The same went for kitchen benchtop wiping (hard cloth *then* soft cloth, twice). Don't even get me started on how I insisted the toilet needed to be cleaned. My husband could never meet my standards (the children were still learning to walk and talk so they were no use). Said husband – previously live-in boyfriend – had been dismissed from laundry folding, kitchen bench wiping, toilet cleaning and many other chores for almost a decade at that point. I realised, while reading Maushart's book, that I was contributing to the problems we were having in fairly sharing housework. Worse, I was creating the problems.

I immediately stopped gatekeeping. In fact, I dropped my standards so low that my husband started complaining about how dirty and messy our house was. In what I think was some sort of attempt to redress the balance, he became a neat and clean freak. During this time, he took a photo of our bedroom. On the floor on his side of the bed was lovely, clean carpet. On the floor on my side were clothes, sunglasses, shoes, mugs, wine glasses, books and all manner of things – piled up to the height of the mattress. Who has time to tidy up when she is becoming a world-famous professor?

You might be relieved to know that I no longer live like a hobo. The housework at our place is shared and the house looks like any typical house that has three adult males coming and going, and a wife/mother/professor who is not interested in carpets, curtains, colours – or dusting. Let's just say we are unlikely to be invited to be the show home in *Sunday Life* or *Modern Living* any time soon.

Sit down and think about whether you have set standards of domestic and/or institutional housework that are unnecessarily high. Be honest with yourself. I bet you have. Ask yourself whether you, too, are gatekeeping and, by doing so, are trapping yourself in circumstances that will use up your time, energy and goodwill on things that are not going to help you – in any way. Then take some action.

Remember the list of things to say no to, stop doing, or stop doing perfectly in Chapter Four? Now I want to give you a stretch assignment. Try doing one thing at level five or six out of 10. Just one housework task each at home and at work. Note what happens. If civilisation does begin to collapse, go right back to folding the laundry to high-end designer-shop standards or answering every email you are sent within minutes. Otherwise, use the time you save to rest, reset and focus on the things that count.

Remember when I told you about marrying my husband because he can cook and that he does all the cooking? (It was about the time you went off me for a bit.) It might help you to like me again to know that the standards in the cooking department in our house have, at times, been very low indeed. When I was a Level B and my husband worked in a corporate environment that required long hours, I cooked for the family for a period of time. I'm happy to report that no-one died as a result of my poor housewifery in the kitchen.

However, Gourmet Central it was not. One night, I made dhal and rice. My then nine-year-old, Aengus, was happily eating his dinner at the kitchen bench when he suddenly piped up, 'Mum, this dinner is amazing!' I spun around from where I was serving myself from the stove and asked, 'Really?' This was a highly unusual comment about my cooking. His eyes were shining. 'Yes!' he said. He explained, 'I'm eating the dhal and it has absolutely NO TASTE. And then I'm eating the rice and IT has absolutely NO TASTE either. So altogether,' he said, gesturing with his fork in a circle to the whole plate, 'this dinner has absolutely NO TASTE. It's AMAZING!' He happily finished his dinner. I'm pleased to report that he is now a six-foot, two-inch 22-year-old, healthy young man who has almost finished a university degree. See? Hard evidence that being bad at housework can not only do no harm, it can even lead to great things. Not to mention a great story.

My dhal and rice was about a one out of ten (the score of one being for the wonder it created in my nine-year-old's mind about how food could have absolutely no taste). Civilisation continued and I became a professor and a senior deputy vice-chancellor and senior vice-president. No-one will stand at my funeral and lament my terrible housewifery.

The final thing I'll say about cooking as the example of housework at home that you could start doing badly is this: baked beans on toast *is* a meal. I asked a dietitian once and she agreed. OK, technically, she wasn't fully qualified as a *dietitian* and she gave a long, complicated answer about complementary proteins or some such, and I stopped listening, but in essence she did not disagree, as far as I heard. I rest my case.

At work, try not doing the institutional housework you normally do to 'oil the wheels' – whether it be note taking in a team meeting, action item follow-ups from meetings, reminders to colleagues who you have correctly predicted will forget important things, check-ins with everyone to monitor their wellbeing, popping the 11 cups and 14 knives and 37 teaspoons lying in the sink into the dishwasher and wiping the bench in the shared kitchen every day, remembering birthday cards, organising morning teas, and so on.

Try dialling down the quality of the work housework that must be done to a five, six or seven out of ten. If you must answer emails, force yourself to send minimal responses (a time to NOT maximise) or to not answer some emails *at all*. *Ever.* Just delete them. I'm confident you will be able to choose which emails, and from whom, to ignore. I bet you'll find this slightly thrilling and wildly liberating – particularly if you are usually a good girl. I so enjoy deleting emails.

Now watch what happens. First, look out the window and see if Earth has continued to turn. All good? Check the hallways/Zoom screen and out the window – is civilisation still operating and not collapsing? Great. Now see who notices whatever you've done badly first (I bet it's no-one). Watch

what happens next. I warn you that this might be quite a dull exercise as it's likely not much will happen at all. Now use the time, energy and goodwill you have saved, and will continue to save, to focus on the things that count for your advancement.

In my defence, I love a birthday morning tea at work. In fact, I am the one who has introduced compulsory morning teas for birthdays when I start in a new place and they aren't normal practice. I'm not a bad person who doesn't care about people or social interactions at work. But I make the person having the birthday bring their own cake (genius, if I do say so – especially given my lack of talent in the kitchen) and everyone brings their own coffee/tea. Then I boss everyone into helping clean up. ('Bill, get back in here and take your plate to the kitchen – we don't have a maid!' Bill is always sneaking off at clean-up time because he doesn't want to get cake icing on his suit.)

Conclusion

You have defined success and it does *not* include winning an award for 'Having the World's Most Sparkly Bathroom' or, 'The Answering All of the Emails From Every Student in First Year in Record Time Using Full Sentences Award'. You know that you need to do more of what counts and less of what does not count. You have started to raise your profile and made keeping it high a priority. You have an achievements file set up and may have already put some entries in there. You will be detailing the evidence of your impact. You will be maximising your head off. If you're a mother, you're aware that your kids will not remember 97.4 percent* of what you have done for them, and have already started doing less for them. You have stopped hand-making playdough and bought a slab of cans of baked beans. You have a clear focus on what you need to do to get promoted and started putting that plan together. You need time and energy to put in an outstanding application. To do that I now again urge you to make 'no' your favourite word and be the worst at housework that you can possibly be – you beating the odds depends on it.

What's coming up?

There is a lot to do. You can't – and don't need to – do this alone. You'll need a support squad. And that's what the next chapter is about.

---

* I estimated this from my own experience (yes, OK, I made it up). It could be higher in your case.

CHAPTER SIX

Form a Support Squad

Becoming a squad leader

To advance in academia, there's a lot you need to do on your own. But there's more that will require input from others. This chapter is about the support squad that you will need to help you succeed. I call this collection of individuals a 'squad' even though most of them will never meet each other and perhaps none of them even know they are in the squad.

Consciously assemble – in your mind – all of the professional and personal supporters you have in your life. There – your squad is formed. This serves a number of purposes. First, it helps you identify who you know in your life who can help you to beat the odds while concurrently remaining upright and sane, and having a ready list to call on. Second, it can be comforting on dark days and in difficult times to recall that this large number of people care about you, your success and/or your wellbeing. Third, putting your squad together is a fun exercise and we all need more fun in our lives. Fourth, guys do this all the time to help each other – it's called the boys' network or the boys' club. Fortunately, creating, building and nurturing support is something at which women often excel, even if they don't realise it. Forming a support squad will likely be easy for you.

Advancing in academia is not a solo pursuit for anyone, and especially not for women. You must create and nurture systems that will sustain and support you, as well as provide key inputs into your career decision-making. You will need a large squad of people to support you over many years as you pursue your goal of advancing in academia, which will include professional supporters and personal supporters. You will also need to be a key member of your own support team and build your personal resilience, which I will

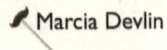
Marcia Devlin

explain further below. Membership of your squad will be rolling, with new members being added as needed and some dropping off as your life, needs and goals change. All of your supporters will be engaged in assisting you to meet your academic or professional advancement goals and broader definitions of success.

Professional support

Professional support comes in many forms and from many sources. Below I briefly outline the support you need and can garner from work colleagues, confidantes, your line manager, senior leaders, mentors, coaches and sponsors.

Work colleagues

Look inside and outside your institution for work colleagues who can assist your advancement – as well as make your daily life far more enjoyable than would otherwise be the case. They can be in similar, complementary or completely different roles to yours. For example, as an academic, I have usefully made deep connections with many colleagues in so-called 'third space' roles in university libraries, student support roles and research leadership roles. Outside universities, I am connected to third-party agencies, a range of professional associations and peak bodies, and to media contacts, among others. Be expansive and creative in your thinking about who to include in your support squad.

Time and effort spent creating and maintaining relationships with work colleagues is almost always both win-win and worthwhile. Being able to interact with intelligent, engaged colleagues around issues of mutual interest can make the difference between a job you enjoy and one that is merely tolerated or endured. Many colleagues I have had over my career have become personal friends. Colleagues can help you navigate academia, politics and the workplace – and provide both personal as well as professional support. While in the previous few chapters I have tried to convince you to help others less, in the case of peers and other colleagues, I would encourage exceptions. For example, offering to assist with interview panels, reviews of various kinds and – careful to avoid over-commitment – a committee and working group for a limited time, can be the beginning of a mutually beneficial professional relationship. It can also lead to the inclusion of a number of welcome additions to your support squad.

Work confidantes

Work confidantes are the colleagues that you trust. You might only have one or two of these colleagues in your workplace, or you might not have any –

they can be rare creatures. Part-colleague, part-friend, a work confidante is ethical and principled and will never push you under a metaphorical bus. They will certainly never participate in gossiping about you and will, instead, have your back – and you will have theirs. These delightful human beings are precious, and your relationship must be protected, no matter what else is going on. Women often excel at developing and maintaining these relationships. You are probably already all over this. But a word of warning: if there is even a skerrick of doubt, do not put your trust in a work colleague and make them a confidante. Academic workplaces and the politics that accompany them can be brutal – be careful.

Line managers
A female keynote speaker at a conference I attended once recommended to the audience of emerging female leaders that they choose their leaders carefully. This advice struck me. Before I heard this woman speak, I had never thought of myself as having any agency in terms of who my line manager was. I was too busy crossing my fingers and hoping the person I reported to was nice – and trying my best to be a good girl so that he (it has most often been a he) would like me. This conference speaker talked about the need for women to do due diligence, including interviewing your potential future line manager (while you were being interviewed for a role), and making conscious decisions about whether or not you wanted to work with and report to this person.

I have both taken this advice on board and ignored it at different times in my career. When I ignored my instincts about someone who I suspected would be narcissistic and selfish as a leader, she (unfortunately, yes, she) turned out to be even worse than I had imagined. Working for her was a living nightmare. At another time, when I overestimated my ability to tolerate a weak, vain and self-centred man as my line manager, I ended up having to choose between breaching my principles and ethics and leaving my job. I chose the latter, which allowed me to live the way I wanted to, in one sense, but I was without a job for a period of time.

*You may think you have no choice about a reporting line. There is **always** a choice.*

Your line manager will have a significant impact on your career. If they support, mentor, coach and/or sponsor you, you have a far greater chance of beating the odds. If they are ambivalent, you'll probably do OK if you manage them well. But if the person you report to is focused on their own glorious

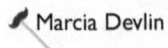

future and only interested in how you can help them, things can be much more difficult. Worse, if you have a nasty, pernicious leader intent on either using you to get ahead or on deliberately holding you back – I've had more than one – they can cause you damage. You may think you have no choice about a reporting line. There is *always* a choice, although the options may be unpalatable. Make your choices mindfully and carefully.

Senior leaders

Universities operate on hierarchies. It will help your career to have connections to one or more senior leaders in your own institution and in others. These people can provide advice, opportunities and references (and opportunities to name drop!). I was appointed to one role because I got to know a senior person while doing voluntary work on a conference committee. I started as a casual and became an ongoing staff member. I also had a chair position created for me to apply for by a vice-chancellor who saw me present at a conference. Review the advice in the last chapter about your profile and, especially, how you might get on the radar of senior people – it can't hurt you. Having senior people in your support squad will most likely help you a lot.

You can seek advice from senior women, bearing in mind that they are busy, and if they are senior, they have got there partly by frequently saying no. There are many ways to ask though, besides an email asking someone you have never met to mentor you (don't do this). Be creative. For example, when I was on maternity leave and subsequently when I was working part-time (for what felt like 150 years), I attended seminars and talks by female professors. I went to sessions on any topic – engineering, chemistry, bugs – you name it, I was there. I attended sessions on topics about which I knew nothing and (to be honest) in which I had absolutely no interest.

I'd sit near the front and at the end while she was packing up, I would approach the speaker. I would ask her whether I could seek her advice. I'd quickly explain my situation of being a mother of young children and then ask her if she had any advice about managing kids and a career. And take away whatever gem she gave me. If she was particularly friendly and interested in talking to me, I'd ask her how old her youngest child was when she went back to work full-time. I asked lots of women this question. The answer was eight years old, in case you are interested. The week Aengus turned eight, I went back to full-time work. For us as a family, it was perfect timing and worked out well. You might have another creative idea about how to trick senior women into giving you advice. I will look forward to hearing from you when you try your trick on me.

Mentors

Mentors are wonderful. They can share their experiences and perspectives, act as trusted advisers, and be available as a sounding board and/or to debrief and give you valuable advice. Mentors can help you navigate sexism and all of the related obstacles you will meet on your path in academia. You can benefit from senior female mentors in particular because they have trodden the path you are on. But mentors are not a panacea. They are not responsible for the management of your career or your career decisions – nor should they be. They also may not be able to assist with some of the circumstances in which you find yourself. That said, it is usually helpful to have mentors.

> *I try to have five to six mentors – some of whom can double as referees – at any time.*

You may notice I used 'mentors' and not 'a mentor' above. That was deliberate. It is unusual to find everything you seek from a mentor in one person. Instead, a range of mentors and advisers are often more helpful. One might specialise in how to improve your research, another in managing tricky political situations, and yet another in navigating having children and succeeding at work. I try to have five to six mentors – some of whom can double as referees – at any time. It's part of my annual strategy. This takes a lot of deliberate, strategic work but is absolutely worth the time and effort.

At one point, when I was a senior lecturer, I targeted and deliberately set about establishing and maintaining relationships with six female professors. For example, one showed a slight interest in something I had done that she had heard about, and I jumped on this interest and began corresponding with her. She wrote back. I played it cool but kept in touch. After a few months, I asked her if I could buy her lunch and seek some career advice. She was delighted. I now consider that person a friend and she continues to provide career advice as well as friendship. She always seems delighted to hear from me and has kept in touch too, so I assume our relationship has some benefits for her as well. Regardless of how she feels, she is in my support squad!

Another mentor early in my career asked how my PhD was going, so I sent her a brief update. A few months later, I sent another brief update. A little while later, I asked her for advice on a particular aspect of my work about which I knew she knew something – which I may or may not have learned through semi-stalking this woman (by which I mean finding out absolutely everything I possibly could about her and her work to inform my strategy to engage with her). Over a coffee, she once shared something small about her personal life with me. I made sure to ask her about that, and about herself, every time we talked or emailed. I wanted to make sure that I offered at least a little in return for what I was getting from her. Most of us appreciate someone asking after us and remembering details of our lives – and mentors are no different.

By the way, these women – and, indeed, most of my mentors – do not know they are my mentors. The first one has already asked for a copy of this book, and I wonder if she will recognise herself in the paragraph above. I don't refer to these two women or any of my mentors as mentors. There has never been a formal or informal discussion, or any arrangements made around them mentoring me. In each case, the relationship evolved through actions such as those I have described above.

You might find what I have described a bit perturbing. You might think 'semi-stalking' (or any stalking) is not the right thing to do. You might think what I have done seems manipulative. You might think instead that being a good girl and waiting patiently to be discovered is a better option. If so, re-read the section in Chapter Four about making plans. I can almost guarantee that no-one will magically discover you sitting quietly in your office and sponsor your career (more about sponsors and mentors below). If you want to beat the odds, you need to give up on being a good girl, and instead get an attitude, be strategic and deliberate, raise your profile, focus on what counts, say no more often and be bad at housework. Then go find potential mentors, and facilitate and maintain relationships with them. Rather than thinking of it as 'manipulation', think of it as 'networking', 'engagement' and 'influencing'. Rather than 'stalking', it is 'background reading'.

Coaches

If mentors are wonderful, coaches are sensational. If you are serious about advancing as a woman in academia, I recommend employing a professional coach, at least for a period or periods of time while you work toward a specific goal or through a difficult situation. The first thing most women think when this is suggested is, 'I can't afford a coach.' While I understand this thinking, and followed it myself for many years, things really changed when I finally employed a coach. Based on my experience, there are a few opposing arguments to 'I can't afford it' that I'd like to put forward:

1. Employing a coach is an investment, not a cost. Once you get promoted or a new higher-level role and/or a bonus, you will double or triple your investment in little time. You might even be able to

claim it as a tax deduction. **YOU SHOULD NOT TAKE THIS AS TAX ADVICE AND SHOULD INSTEAD ASK A QUALIFIED ACCOUNTANT ABOUT THIS.** Sorry to shout, but I don't want you to sue me and eat into my book profits.
2. You probably pay a hairdresser a small fortune annually to make your hair look nice, yet your fabulous hair (or fabulous shoes, or fabulous other things you spend money on) will have a neutral impact on your career advancement. A coach will help you to advance. By the way, I'm not against hairdressers (and mine is sensational – see the section on personal support) nor against shoes. Mmmmmmm, shoes.
3. If you want to beat the odds, investing in a coach focused on helping you succeed is a strategic move. She/he will help you choose the appropriate attitudes, define success, strategise and plan, set and meet goals, focus on what counts, succeed at saying no and be the worst at housework the world has ever seen.
4. If you haven't had a coach, you don't know what you are missing out on. Having a coach has been one of the top three things that has helped me succeed in my career. They are brilliant.
5. It's excellent to have someone in your life whose job and focus is to help you and nothing else. You feel for a short time each month that it's all about you and that is a rare and lovely feeling as a woman.
6. You're worth it.

I've had a few coaches. I've found each of them useful in different ways – and some more than others. One recommended I 'create spaces and opportunities for myself'. I had no idea what that meant. I asked her. She said, 'Think about it.' (She was a bit annoying at times – I mean, I'm paying her, and she won't explain what she means.) But I did think about it. I thought and thought. I wrote the advice down on a piece of paper and stared at it. I stuck the piece of paper on my noticeboard and stared at it. My husband asked me what it meant. I said I didn't know and asked him if he knew. He looked at me strangely and said, 'It's in your handwriting, Marcia,' then left the room. I turned it into an acronym – CSAOFM. I stared at that too. Nothing.

Then one day, in the shower (where we all know the best thinking happens), I remembered a colleague from several years previously who had tried and failed to talk me into applying for a Telstra Business Women's Award. She was a fellow professor at the same university, but in a different department. A well-respected, highly published professor who had become Telstra Business Woman of the Year while in a previous role in another state. She had dragged me along to Telstra Business Women breakfasts and various

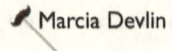

other events held for these awardee alumni for years. She had tried and failed to point out that I ran a 'business', with my 250-member university-wide research group at the time we worked together.

As I started to go prune-like in the shower, I began to consider applying for one of these awards. That would be a space/opportunity for me, perhaps. It would save me the embarrassment of having to report that I had not done my homework when I next met my coach. Long story short, I did apply – based on my work at a regional university creating and implementing a digital strategy for learning and teaching, another strategy on opening access to a wider range of students and a third around retaining and facilitating success for equity group students. I was honoured as a state finalist for Telstra Business Woman of the Year. My professor friend sat proudly at my table at the gala event, alongside my husband, my two sons and my parents. I met an amazing new network of women outside my usual networks – some of whom I am still in touch with many years later, and from whom I have learned much and continue to be inspired by.

The process of applying was thorough and rigorous, and it gave me the opportunity to reflect on my career, impact, principles and plans. I subsequently applied for two more awards – one each at state and national level – that were run by two separate organisations. I won both awards, again widening my horizons and networks while being exposed to different perspectives, as well as adding lines to my CV that contributed to me continuing to advance in academia.

Having a coach has been one of the top three things that has helped me succeed in my career. They are brilliant.

The coach led me to think outside the box – to create spaces and opportunities for myself – and this led to me growing and advancing as a professional. I wish I had found a coach earlier and believed and invested in myself as an up-and-coming academic. It would have sped up my path and helped me realise earlier what counted and what did not count.

I used a coach to help me write this book – a book coach. I would never have finished it otherwise. I've started a few books and my computer is littered with half- and quarter-written tomes. I write a lot and have a lot of publications, but I appear to have the attention span of a gnat when it comes to longer pieces of writing. Chapters and refereed articles are hard enough for me – I prefer writing short media articles. I found a book coach, engaged her, followed her instructions and here I am towards the end – confident this book will be finished soon and see the light of day soon after.

I highly recommend you consider engaging a coach. You are definitely worth it.

Sponsors

If you are one of the rare and fortunate few, you may be able to experience having a sponsor for your career or part of your career. Note that I did not say you may be able to 'find' a sponsor. Usually, sponsors find you, not the other way around. To be found, you need to have a profile that makes you findable and impressive. Your work cannot speak for itself – you have to help it speak, loudly and clearly.

If you want to improve your chances of being sponsored, there's a great guide on the Universities Australia website that will help you understand more about sponsorship[33]. In collaboration with another female executive colleague, I commissioned this guide while we were national co-chairs of Universities Australia Executive Women (now called Universities Australia Women). You could even print this off and anonymously mail it to every member of the executive team at your university. Keep your expectations in check, though, as they may not read it and you will probably never know. Just after it was published, I gave a copy to every male executive colleague who visited my office. One left it on the table when he gathered up his stuff to leave after our meeting. I handed it to him again as he arranged his things. 'For you,' I said, smiling. I don't know for sure, but judging by how little support he provided for the women who reported to him, he probably never opened it.

The importance of professional support

You may feel you don't have time to build and maintain relationships with professional colleagues. Your workload and other responsibilities are such that these relationships are not a priority. I understand how hard it is to find yet more time in an already crowded schedule to engage in what can feel like a waste of time. But while not every single effort you make to build or improve a relationship will have a direct impact on your advancement, having a sound group of people in your professional network on whom you can lean is critical to your success in academia. If you don't believe me about the importance of professional contacts, perhaps you will believe Australia's only female prime minister. Julia Gillard says in her most recent book[34] that looking back on her time as a politician, she realises she should have made

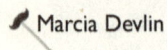
Marcia Devlin

more effort to broaden her networks and build new coalitions – for all the benefits these can bring in good times and bad.

You might doubt my advice here. After all, the number of professional contacts you have will not be directly measured as part of a promotion application. And some of the people you admire will appear to be 'flying solo' and achieving great outcomes on their own. But behind every successful woman in academia is a squad of professional supporters – whether they know they are in the squad or not. If you are reluctant, select a small number of people with whom you would like to connect, or who you would like to strengthen your connection with. Add a stream to your advancement strategy and plans, with actions you can take to make or improve this connection. Determine whether these actions will include following them on social media and/or liking their posts, sending them a message about a topic of mutual interest, asking for their advice on something in their area of expertise, complimenting them on an achievement or something else. Relationships take time to create and deepen, so make sure you give this the time it will need.

You may feel you are too introverted to take action in this area. I say (as an extrovert) that introverts are smarter than extroverts – and you can and will find a way. We extroverts are busy doing all the talking and working out what we think as we say it. If you are thinking more deeply about things, as introverts tend to do, you could probably give the extroverts some advice about how to improve the many surface-level relationships we have.

When I was a senior deputy vice-chancellor, I made a point of funding women to attend leadership professional development. When I asked how this development opportunity had helped, one shared the following by email:

> *What I was not expecting, and what surprised me the most, was seeing how the right 'safe' environment can quickly break through our years of acquired (required) 'protective wear', freeing vulnerabilities and opening us up to frank and honest sharing of experiences, knowledge and ideas. The realisation was quite simply – we (women) are stronger together. Clearly this is not a massive revelation, but for me, it kind of was. Even though I've collaborated with many wonderful, smart, funny, confident women over the years, I would say this was the first time that I truly felt a part of the collective power of my women colleagues.*
>
> *I guess what I wish I had known/realised earlier in my career, was the strength, power and insight that I could*

> gain and give, if I had only got out of my discipline-
> bubble. By staying in my bubble, flying solo to a large
> extent, honing my expertise that would (hopefully) see me
> rewarded with a new contract or career progression, it
> meant I was susceptible to career isolation and the belief
> that my career was in the hands of others.

Ensuring you have professional support in all the ways outlined above will help you beat the odds. Personal support will also help you.

Personal support

Succeeding in academia is hard. It can use up most of our time and energy, and eat away at our store of goodwill. The environment we are in is tough and demanding. It is key to have a life outside of academia and have people in our personal lives who support us. These people help us meet our personal definition of success – which hopefully includes goals outside of work – and they make our lives richer. Has there ever been a time in recent history as powerful as the current global pandemic in underscoring for us all the unique and wonderful value of human connection and interaction? Having a personal support squad is a delightful and increasingly necessary part of your success strategy.

You can't have too much personal support

You might think you have enough personal support. I recommend you up the ante if you want to advance in academia. The odds – and forces – are against you. My experience tells me that if you stop being a good girl, you are going to get into trouble. When you get into trouble, you are going to need personal resilience and people to turn to. In my career, I have failed to meet gendered expectations many times and have definitely not been a good girl. I have been subjected to a number of 'style' conversations – and much, much worse. My personal support squad has been the difference between me recovering to continue thriving in our environment and, frankly, me leaving academia. I know many women who have also rejected the good girl expectations who say similar things. We'll talk more about what to do when things go wrong at work in the next chapter. In the meantime, I have a bit of an unusual take on personal support that I would like to share with you.

The personal support I have needed as an academic has differed depending on my stage of life, my circumstances and the ages of my children.

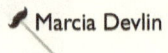
Marcia Devlin

That said, at all stages and ages, my female peers have been my lifeline and the most important sources of support.

Personal support people know how to listen and when to offer just enough encouragement.

When my children were babies, the women with whom I did mothers group and playgroup were women who understood my situation, were completely non-judgemental and offered me unconditional support. The relationships I had with these women meant the difference, for me, between enjoying life with babies while maintaining a career connection and suffering through life with babies while giving up on my academic career. We had a lot of fun.

Progressing in one's academic career is a lot of hard slog, so having fun is a good counterbalance. More than once with my playgroup mothers, I drank champagne at 10 o'clock in the morning and smoked cigarettes, even though I didn't smoke. We laughed and cried together and shared intimacies (in addition to the irresponsible drinking and smoking) that seem quite shocking when looking back. But these women got me through that stage and helped me appreciate it. When I took my first tentative steps back to work after maternity leave, with a baby who didn't sleep more than three hours in a row, they helped me figure out what to wear on the first day, how to get a cheap haircut that didn't look cheap, and cheered me on through the constant challenges of balancing poor sleep, young children and keeping up the façade of professionalism.

Later, the primary school mothers played a similar role until the high school mothers took over, alongside my book group friends with whom I still meet regularly. We rarely talk about the book – sometimes to the chagrin of the more serious members who actually want to read books. For me, it's a support group I would be lost without. They give me a joyous experience every six weeks, discussing literature and life and giving me the opportunity to forget about work at the same time.

Personal support people know how to listen and when to offer just enough encouragement without trying to solve all of our problems with their advice. The good supporters know how to *just be* with adversity—calming us rather than frustrating us. When things go wrong, they give us the space to grieve and to work through our emotions.

Watch out for frenemies

However, not all friends are friendly. One woman who participated in a development program I ran for female staff at one university lived in a small community. She mentioned that when she spoke about work with her friends from when she was at school, they took little interest and did not seem supportive. When she gently broached the subject with a smaller group of these closest friends, they complained she was 'always talking about work'. A little embarrassed by this feedback, she monitored their conversations for a while, contributing less than she had done previously and listening more. She told me that she then noticed her friends' conversations were limited and focused on their children, the evening meal and gossiping about other people in their community. She told me she didn't feel supported by her friends in her career aspirations and, given she wanted to follow my advice about leaning on friends for support, asked what I thought she should do. I didn't hesitate: 'Get new friends.'

This might seem harsh and even shocking, but my view of the relationships was the one this colleague eventually came to as well – these so-called friends were not supporting her in her goals for her career and life, and did not deserve a spot in the squad. When I bumped into this colleague a few months later, she told me she was still friendly with these women she had grown up with but had begun to develop new friends at work and in the industry aligned with her discipline area. She told me the new friends had goals and ambitions that aligned with her own, unlike her old friends. She told me she was already feeling more supported by these new friends.

Most women also know about the 'frenemy'. This is another woman we have in our life who is supposed to be a friend but, through a range of means, operates more like an enemy. She might be a little too pleased when we have failures or disappointments, keen to counter any good news we share with better news of her own, or just a little bit too critical of us. The bottom line is that she makes us feel worse for having seen her, rather than better. You don't have time for this so give her a wide berth and, if necessary, kick her off your support squad.

Who is in your squad?

I have a squad of supporters in my personal life. They include my husband, my sons, my mother, a small number of close friends, my book group friends, a wider circle of friends, exercise buddies, some of my neighbours and a collection of health and beauty professionals. I realise I might have lost some of you again at this last point. I admit this is an unusual take on the usual advice to women that they should network. Bear with me.

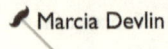
Marcia Devlin

My personal support crew includes my hairdresser, Luke, who has been there for every significant event in my life in the past 10 years – including the nights I won awards and the day I attended my father's funeral. He is my hair stylist, amateur psychologist and friend. He knows everything about my life – and if you have been awful to me at work, Luke knows about it (take *that*). I have a massage therapist, Paul, who regularly untangles the ever-present knots in my shoulders and neck – all the time speaking in soothing tones. I have an osteopath, Rob, who works in tandem with Paul to try to put things back in place when my long hours at the computer and terrible posture play havoc with my back. I see my naturopath, Jan, regularly and she asks me 100 questions about my lifestyle, and prescribes herbs, exercise and lifestyle adjustments to address whatever needs my body (and mind) has. I recently acquired a physio, Rees, who is treating my COVID injury in my hip (walking too much). I have a neighbour and friend, Jane, who is also my lawyer and with whom I walk sometimes and always call first in a crisis. I have a psychologist, Robyn – formerly in Melbourne, now in Tasmania – who provides Skype sessions whenever I need them. I also have a great female doctor I see when I need to and a lovely optometrist I visit once or twice a year.

I'm aware that all of this health and beauty care may make me sound like a princess. I don't care. These personal supporters are part of my support squad and they all play a part in helping me survive and thrive in my career. By the way, none of these people know they are members of my squad – this all happens in my head. Well, except Luke because I tell him everything. And more recently Paul because we chat a lot. And now the book is progressing well, I've also told Rob. And I'm about to tell Rees at my next physio appointment because his wife is an academic and he's already pre-ordered a copy of this book for her based on its subject matter alone, but you get my point. I highly recommend you create and nurture a similar squad – it's great fun.

You might feel you do not have the resources necessary to put into a large number of personal relationships. You might prefer to go with what you have, which may be a small and strong group of personal supporters. That is fine, but you could easily expand this group and lose nothing from it by thinking about people already in your life differently.

Your supporters are everywhere

You may not have a partner, a family who are any help, a book group, friends from school, close friends or a regular hairdresser, massage therapist, osteopath, physiotherapist, lawyer, psychologist, doctor or optometrist. But there are people in your life who you see from time to time, who are part of your community and who you can secretly include in your personal support squad. For example, there's a guy who lives in my neighbourhood who I often see walking around the local park when I am doing the same. He is a delightful human being and always greets me warmly, even if we pass each other three or four times on the same walk as we circle in opposite directions. That guy (I don't know his name) is in my support squad. He will never know he is. But that doesn't matter because he lifts me up and improves my day every time I see him. When I have had terrible days at work and am stomping, rather than walking, around the park, he gives his usual greeting and, by doing so, he supports me.

I also see an old man, Enzo, who lives in my street, once every couple of months. We chat about neighbourhood house prices (he owns multiple houses in our street), his nephew and his family (also my neighbours), and/or whatever is topical or current for 10 or 15 minutes at a time, then go on our way. Each interaction is lovely. Enzo even helped my husband and I decide whether or not to sell our house at one point, even though we don't know his last name. Enzo is in my squad.

Do any of your health or beauty care providers have potential to join your squad? Check out the staff at cafés or eateries you visit regularly or from time to time. Are they potential support squad members? Any nice neighbours? Are the local post office staff friendly? Do you have a current acquaintance who you might want to get to know a little better? Another parent at the kids' school? Or are there people already in your life who you could turn to a little more?

Perhaps, when you think about your support squad, it seems a little weak. No need to panic. Just start to put people in place, one by one. Consciously put effort into those relationships now you realise how important they are. It will do you no harm to try it – it's all in your head anyway.

At the beginning of this chapter, I mentioned the importance of supporting yourself, and, specifically, building your personal resilience. The next section explains the importance of putting effort into developing this critical attribute.

Personal resilience

You are probably good at supporting others – your partner, children, relatives, friends, colleagues. To succeed in academia, you need to learn to support yourself as one of your top priorities.

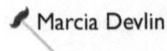
Marcia Devlin

The interrelated skills of building, maintaining and drawing on your resilience are key to being a successful female in higher education. Demonstrating resilience is one of the major reasons I have made it to the top of the academic and senior executive hierarchy in academia. While your support squad will be enormously helpful, you are going to have to rely heavily on yourself as well to get through the tough times. In particular, you are going to have to be resilient.

What is resilience?

The specific concept of resilience is about the ability to recover or 'bounce back' from challenges and difficulties. We all know people who are really good at doing this; for example, something terrible happens in their life and they somehow manage to get over it and move forward. We also all know people who are not resilient – something goes wrong, it floors them, and they either can't recover or struggle to do so. But resilience is a skill you can learn, although it does need to be practised. If you want to be a senior woman in higher education, you would benefit from learning and practising it.

Having resilience means you are better able to protect yourself against harmful or overwhelming experiences, and to maintain balance in your life – be that at work or more broadly. It doesn't mean you don't suffer when bad things happen, but it does mean you are less likely to remain trapped in that suffering, and that you can recover and return to normal or a new normal – and do so relatively quickly.

Using resilience to manage challenges and advance your career

If you are a woman in academia and, instead of being a good girl, you are swimming against the tide of gendered expectations, implicit associations, being invisible, benevolent sexists, not-so-benevolent sexists, nice-guy misogynists, not-so-nice-guy misogynists, manterruptions, bro-propriation, assumptions you will bake the cupcakes, choose the carpets, curtains and colours, and care for the children and others as well as being nice and nurturing with the correct amount of humility and the 'right' style, then you are definitely going to run into trouble. Big trouble. There is no way, as far as I can see, for you to reject these 'business-as-usual' expectations without some blowback, repercussions, slapdowns, payback or some other form of serious trouble.

> *Building and having resilience is an ongoing endeavour, rather than a one-off in response to a difficult situation.*

In my career, I have tolerated and managed being gossiped about, lied about, disparaged, bullied, mobbed, threatened, gaslighted, ostracised, pushed out of roles and worse. From my experience and from supporting countless female colleagues in theirs, getting into trouble is going to hurt. A lot. If it is really bad, you may feel like you have been knocked sideways, that you are smashed or broken, that you cannot breathe and, at times, like you cannot go on. Resilience will help you.

Building and having resilience is an ongoing endeavour, rather than a one-off in response to a difficult situation. Here is a summary of how I manage these sorts of challenges.

First, I try to adopt an accepting attitude. After 30 years as a woman in academia, I understand and know that I – and other women – will have challenging, unfair, sometimes outrageous things happen, and I accept this is inevitable. This doesn't mean you or I lie down and let people walk over us. In my case, it doesn't mean I don't have strong revenge fantasies against people who undermine, intimidate or hurt me – believe me, I do – but I don't act on them. Instead, I accept that poor and bad behaviour from others is par for the course on a female's journey in academia and that being on the receiving end of it is often stressful. I also accept that it is preferable to acknowledge the truth, and any associated pain, than it is to ignore it, repress it or deny it.

Second, I have created a self-care menu of things that build my resilience. I have written this out, stuck it to a private noticeboard at home and refer to it frequently to remind myself about what helps me be and stay strong. Your list will be different to mine, but here are some suggestions to get you started. Among other things, I:

- exercise regularly;
- try to eat a reasonably healthy diet (I argue ice-cream is made from dairy, which has calcium in it so it's basically a healthy choice);
- try to get enough sleep, or at least enough rest;
- keep a journal (irregularly);
- spend time with people who make me laugh;
- try to maintain a sense of humour;
- enjoy time on my own;

- sit on my front porch with a cup of tea and watch the leaves of the trees in my street moving in the breeze;
- listen to music I enjoy;
- savour and feel gratitude for all that is good in my life;
- practise meditation (I'm terrible, but I keep trying);
- watch series and comedy on streaming services;
- avoid ugly people (I mean the ones who are terrible humans); and
- try to deliberately have compassion for others, including those who are awful to me (I'm very, very bad at this and I don't want to do it anymore but the experts say it's a good thing to do).

I have found that good relationships and company are vital to building and maintaining resilience. Resilient people keep good company. They seek out and surround themselves with other resilient people – whether just for fun, or when there's a need for support. Hence the support squad idea.

My resilience is also strengthened through books. Novels and literature in general give me great insight into how others manage and live their lives, and resolve issues. I also find nonfiction helpful. For example, when my children were very young, Susan Maushart's *The Mask of Motherhood*[35] left me speechless with relief. It talks about the idealisation of motherhood and mothers, and how we have to pretend we are sweetness and light and children are presents from heaven for which we are forever grateful – *when that's not really how many of us feel*. Before I read her book, I thought there was something wrong with me. Afterwards, I knew there was at least one person in the world who understood how I felt. I hope this book is providing some of the same sort of comfort and normalisation of your experiences and feelings as a woman working in a university.

Third, when I do not behave like a good girl (most days) and I suffer payback of some kind, I try to use this as a source of motivation. I am fuelled to write this current book on the basis of the cumulative effect of behaviour from others that is so bad that, if I told you about it, you would simply not believe me. This book is a way to reflect, debrief, help other women who may be suffering in similar ways, get some agency back, and (anonymously, without any identifying details) out the people who have hurt me (take *that*, losers!).

Finally, I try to celebrate successes. I try at the end of each day or two, or at least each week, to review what went well and to congratulate myself. Doing this trains the mind to look for the positive, the success, the silver lining, the way 'out' – rather than to dwell on the negative. All of this helps build, maintain, strengthen and demonstrate resilience.

Is this all really necessary?

You might think I am being overly dramatic – like the doomsdayer filling their bunker with tins of tuna and bottled water – and that things cannot possibly be that bad. You might find some of what I have told you hard to believe at all. If you can get through your career in academia as a woman and make it up as far as you want to go without a single moment of trouble, no-one will be more delighted than me. Please let me know so I can interview you to find out the secret to success and share it widely. So far, I haven't met a senior woman who has sailed up through the hierarchy in universities without trouble. These women probably exist but, if the many hundreds of women I have worked with are anything to go by, the women who have had a smooth path are rare. It is likely things will go wrong for you at some point. At that point, personal resilience will be very useful for you.

> *If you resist the expectations to be a good girl and meet the gendered expectations, you are going to get into trouble, and you are going to need to be resilient.*

You might also think I – and other women – have brought trouble on ourselves. You are right here – we have. We have brought trouble on ourselves by rejecting the ludicrous, infuriating, sexist expectations of us – in other words, we have been bad girls, and we have paid for our audacity, our boldness, our impudence and our alleged disrespect. A senior man once disciplined me because I had 'made' him 'feel dismissed' in a meeting. Actually, I had decided *not to stop speaking* when he manterrupted and spoke over me – as usual – in that particular meeting. Instead, that day, tired of his sexist behaviour, I had had the effrontery to *finish my sentence* (and I may have raised the volume of my voice slightly so people could hear me over the manterruption). The payback for my minor transgression was major. The experience left me feeling shocked and terrible.

Peers who had previously worked for this same man were not surprised when I confided in them. We shared our experiences of having lost respect for him after discovering firsthand his unscrupulous drive to look good at all times, his lack of ethical behaviour and his reckless disregard for the wellbeing of those supposedly in his 'care'. Sharing these confidences helped me enormously as I realised there was a common denominator. I went for a long walk, sat on my front porch with a cup of tea and made the same difficult decision several peers before me had made, which vastly improved

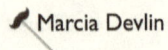
Marcia Devlin

my situation. If you resist the expectations to be a good girl and meet the gendered expectations, you are going to get into trouble, and you are going to need to be resilient.

Resilience does not cure cancer. Repeated or continuous negative experiences cannot be mitigated by a high level of resilience. Nor can resilience be the only tool in your kit. But it will help you when things go wrong, which they are more likely to do if you don't quietly accept the odds.

Make a list of all the activities that help you maintain resilience. Put it somewhere you will see it regularly. Each Friday, when you update your achievements file, look at your resilience actions list and mentally check off which activities you have done this week and which you will try over the weekend and the following week.

Like many things in this book, you might think you don't have time to undertake activities to build your resilience. You might have been right until recently – you have been so busy saying yes to everything and doing all of the housework that you haven't had time for much else. But now you are starting to say no to so many things and do less housework, and do the rest at a six or five out of 10 standard, you may have the time and energy to do some of the things that actually count for advancement. You will need a lot of resilience to make it to the professoriate or into leadership as a woman in academia. Get to it.

What to do when things go wrong

Things have gone wrong for me and for many women I know in universities. Between us we have been variously:

- formally accused of breaching university policy;
- harassed;
- stalked;
- lied about;
- disparaged;
- bullied;
- mobbed;
- gaslighted;
- emailed in the middle of the night;
- denied promotion;
- repeatedly denied access to research funds;
- gossiped about to the point of reputational damage;
- put under performance management for having the 'wrong' style;

- threatened with being removed from our position;
- told our positions had been dissolved while on sick leave in hospital;
- expected to work while seriously ill;
- given no support when family members have life-threatening conditions;
- threatened with legal action;
- threatened with criminal prosecution;
- reminded of the importance of male colleagues' work and feelings; and
- forced to resign.

Some or all of this might be hard for you to believe, especially if you have never experienced, seen or heard of such situations. It is my fervent hope that you retire at the end of a long and successful career without anything like this ever happening to you. But if things do go wrong for you, which is more likely if you take the actions necessary to beat the odds, remember you are not alone and you have prepared for this. You will survive and, with resilience, thrive.

The things that have helped women include drawing on professional and personal support squads, drawing on stores of resilience and using the 4Rs (record, reflect, request, report) from Chapter Five. But there is a negative side to these Rs, which I would like to explain to you now.

In Chapter Five, I told you the 4Rs can help you to have a file of positive evidence on which to draw. But my 4R suggestions are also useful for when you get into trouble and when you are treated inappropriately and poorly.

Record

As well as recording your achievements regularly, I also recommend you make a record of things that do not sit quite right with you. We all have 'icky' interactions, experiences and observations. You have them or observe them, and your instincts tell you something about them is not quite right. Women have a good 'sixth sense' about when things are not quite right. If you feel this way, you may be wrong, but I'll bet you are more often right than wrong.

If you feel icky, write a brief note about what happened and how you felt about what happened. Add a date and file this away. Many of these notes you will never look at again, and that is a good thing. But it is possible there will be a small number of notes you will return to and add to. These records are useful when things go wrong. For example, you might be accused of bullying a colleague – as I and many senior women with the 'wrong' style have been. This is a serious allegation, and if a colleague makes it, they need

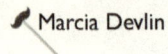
Marcia Devlin

evidence to support their claim. This is likely to come from records they have kept about alleged interactions. It is enormously helpful to have your record of the same interactions to counter false or erroneous claims that are made. I recommend keeping an 'icky feeling' file.

I also have a second file in which I collate emails or other messages that may or may not be related to the records above, but give me the same sense of feeling something is not quite right. They may be overly formal, aggressive, odd in some way or you just sense some games or politics are at play. Trust your gut. If you're wrong, then no harm done in keeping records. If you're right, they can be helpful in a rebuttal, or a counterclaim for harassment or a vexatious claim against you. This happens often to women, and perhaps more so to those who are challenging the expected gendered norms.

Reflect

Review and reflect on these negative records periodically, as you do for the positive records discussed in Chapter Five. This can help you see areas where you need to improve and grow. For example, I noticed at one point that I can hang onto a grudge or tension after I have successfully negotiated a ceasefire with someone with whom I have been sparring. This helped me to change my behaviour and avoid repeating this mistake. Reflecting can also help you see trends and patterns in your experiences, which is enormously helpful. Becoming aware that I was suffering from gendered expectations I had no desire to meet came about partly from deep reflection on records I keep of things that go wrong at work.

Request

When things are not going well and/or you have ongoing uneasy feelings about someone or a situation, request advice. You can do this from any member of your large support squad. In that squad are years of workplace and broader life experience – all of which has the potential to assist you. Show a trusted support squad member your notes and ask them what they think. A colleague recently thought she was being harassed and/or bullied by a colleague and possibly having her rights restricted. She asked me for my honest opinion. I looked at her records and advised my friend she was reading too much into the desperate ramblings of an insecure colleague who was hell-bent on regaining some power she had lost. I advised my colleague to take a break and get some rest to regain her equilibrium and perspective.

If things are highly charged, political, or for some other reason really icky, you can ask your human resources (HR) area for advice. You will get expert, relevant, professional input on your particular circumstances from an internal source who understands your context. By asking for advice on a situation, you have also put something on the record in HR that might later be useful to you. But I must warn you, this doesn't always work.

In one workplace, I had a male colleague who was extremely aggressive toward me. For example, he:

- deliberately excluded me from meetings and communications in which I needed to be included;
- avoided meeting and interacting with me despite the need for us to do so regularly;
- was hostile when he did meet with me;
- refused to make eye contact with me in meetings, including when I was chairing the meeting;
- misrepresented exchanges between us to others, including senior people;
- feigned compliance with agreed actions; and
- made derogatory and sexist comments about me to numerous others.

The latter were based on 'evidence' that was completely fabricated – but were so frequent and widespread, they began to gain traction in some areas. He was so aggressive that after several months of this behaviour, I became frightened to be alone with him. I requested advice from HR. They told me to leave my office door open while meeting with him, stand up while he was sitting at my desk to 'create a different dynamic' and to keep our meetings short*. When taking these actions made little difference to my situation, I sought further advice from my (male) line manager about how to interact with this man. I was advised to 'lavish him with praise – lay it on really thick because he needs *a lot* of praise'. I tried this – to no avail. After about 18 months, when I began to protest about the negative, cumulative impact of his poor behaviour on my mental health, I was repeatedly told by my line manager to 'be the bigger person' in the relationship and to 'rise above his bad behaviour'. Concurrently, I was told I needed to improve my relationship with this hostile, aggressive man who was (literally) making me ill. I did not welcome this direction, nor the responsibility for managing this person's

---

* That's right – they did not suggest his aggressive behaviour should cease, take his aggressive behaviour up with him or his line manager, or in any way address the source of the problem. As far as I know, they didn't have the 'style' conversation with him either.

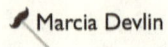
Marcia Devlin

poor behaviour being placed on me. When I sought support from another senior person, I was told, 'The problem with you, Marcia, is your fuckwit management is terrible. You need to get better at managing fuckwits.' You can't make this stuff up.

Don't let this anecdote dissuade you from requesting advice or help. In my case, reflecting on the (lack of appropriate) responses to my requests for advice and help, which I had recorded, helped me to see that the problem lay in the culture and accepted practices of this workplace, and not with me. All of which contributed to my decision to leave this job, which was a great decision.

Report

Report your recordings, reflections and the outcomes of these in appropriate forums. Depending on the nature of the reports and reflections, I have reported them to my line manager, the vice-chancellor, council members and to my lawyer while considering a legal case against a university. You always hope you don't have to go here, but you can consider this if you need to do so and have the requested evidence to back your claims.

Making it past the Hall of Horrors

The list of horrors that befall women in universities is long and shocking. But not every woman experiences every one of these horrors. Some women make it to the top relatively unscathed. In my experience, women with higher levels of patience and tolerance have less trouble than women like me who are outwardly impatient and frustrated with sexism. Those who have stronger skills in diplomacy tend to run into fewer conflicts than women like me, who tend to be candid and outspoken. If you have the qualities that some of my more diplomatic colleagues have, you may fare better than me and some of my other colleagues. I will say that the colleagues who are externally patient, tolerant and diplomatic are often raging inside – they are just more skilled at containing their emotion and channelling it.

If you are not prepared to be a good girl for the entire duration of your career, you should expect things to go wrong and prepare for this eventuality. When they do go wrong, it can be distressing. But it can also be empowering to plan for this. For example, how would you manage finding out a male colleague has said to another colleague that he was 'going to bring you down' (but the reporting colleague does not wish to be identified for fear of reprisal)? This happened to me. What would you do if, in a political attempt to discredit and control you, your (male) line manager raised made-up concerns about your performance you knew were bogus, but he claimed were real? This has happened to a number of women I know. How will you bring in your support squad? Utilise your resilience? What about the 4Rs? Will the false moustache be of any use?

This is upsetting to imagine. Would you be crazy to worry and plan for such appalling behaviour? I don't think so. Think about how you will proactively build and maintain your resilience – a useful life skill anyway – then get to work on that.

Conclusion

In this chapter, I have talked about the importance of having a large and diverse support squad. I have explained how professional colleagues, including work colleagues, confidantes, your line manager, senior leaders, mentors, coaches and sponsors can help you at work in a range of ways. I have explained my unusual approach to a personal support squad, which can be large and diverse and include anyone who you would like to have in your squad. I have talked about the importance of resilience and being able to get back up again after you are inevitably knocked down when you begin to resist the gendered expectations of you. I have also talked about what to do when things go wrong.

You may think you have a good support squad and you don't need to add to that in any way. Perhaps you don't have time anyway. Like all of the suggestions and recommendations I make in this book, the ones I make in this chapter are useful investments in your future. The odds are against you, and you are working in a sexist environment. You need help and you are best placed to arrange that help for yourself. I hope you will consider the ideas in this chapter and make at least some small changes to your support squad and resilience stores to bolster both – this will be time and effort well spent.

What's coming up?

The next chapter reviews the good, the bad and the ugly of beating the odds in academia. It is a call to arms.

CHAPTER SEVEN

Beating the Odds

The good, the bad and the ugly

I started this book with an overview of the good, the bad and the ugly. There is quite a lot in the early sections about how bad (and sometimes ugly) things are for women in universities. Chapters One and Two are pretty depressing. But, hopefully, as you started on Chapter Three and began to progress through the book, you found yourself looking up and feeling better. Hopefully, you found comfort in the anecdotes, ideas, advice, suggestions and recommendations, and in some of the humour.

In this chapter, I'm going to talk about some more good stuff, but also briefly dip in and out of some bad and ugly stuff. I'm trying to reinspire you here with some gravitas. I have used humour to take you through this difficult topic, but I don't want to leave you feeling it's all bright and breezy. I promise to end on good stuff, so bear with me.

Some ugly stuff

Inside and outside universities and across the world, women do not have the same opportunities as men. Not only that, but the 2020 report from the World Economic Forum (WEF) concluded, 'None of us will see gender parity in our lifetimes, and nor likely will many of our children.'[36] The WEF have calculated that gender parity will not be attained for 99.5 years.

The key dimensions used to measure parity are:
- economic participation and opportunity;
- educational attainment;
- health and survival; and
- political empowerment.

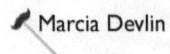
Marcia Devlin

Apart from the obvious fact that a lack of parity is not fair, the report points out that gender parity has a significant bearing on the extent to which economies and societies can thrive. The report adds that deploying only half of the world's available talent has an enormous impact on the growth, competitiveness and future-readiness of businesses and economies across the world. In the Global Gender Gap Index 2020 rankings, included in the WEF report, Australia comes in at number 44. We have slipped five places from the previous year. We have a lower ranking on gender parity than 43 other countries, including some in our region – the Philippines (16th) and New Zealand (6th). This all forms part of the wider context in which Australian universities exist.

Women also get paid less than men across industries and across the world. The 2020 report from the Australian Workplace Gender Equality Agency (WGEA) – a government agency set up to collect data on workplace gender equality indicators – showed that men take home on average $25,534 per year more than women[37]. Contributing to this gap, they found the average, full-time, base salary across all industries and occupations for women is, on average, 15 percent less than the average for men.

One university I worked in had exactly this gender pay gap, and I suspect most universities' gender pay gaps are around the same percentage. The university I worked at took no meaningful action to address the gap, despite the university council having analysed the data and having discussed the matter more than once. That's probably not unusual given the 2020 WGEA finding that, compared to the previous year, there was a significant *reduction* in the number of employers who had analysed the gap who then actually took action to close the gap. There is emerging evidence that the 2020 pandemic has made, and will continue to make, things even worse for women at work, including in universities. This is also part of the context in which Australian universities exist.

More about invisibility

You are probably familiar with the 'glass ceiling' metaphor. It represents an invisible barrier (ceiling) that prevents women from rising beyond a certain level in an organisation's hierarchy. It's operating in every Australian university and only a small proportion of women break through. The 'glass escalator', on the other hand, is a metaphor that refers to the way men fast-track to senior positions in female-dominated professions. Like education, for example. That escalator is in fine working order in Australian universities.

Then there is the 'glass cliff' I mentioned in Chapter Four – the phenomenon of women being more likely than men to achieve leadership roles during periods of crisis or downturn, when the chance of failure is highest. Research by Michelle Ryan and Alexander Haslam, who coined this term, shows women are more often elevated to positions of power when things are not going well for the organisation[38]. They then have a higher likelihood of failure, meaning there's a greater risk for them to fall off the invisible 'cliff'. It is my prediction that partly because of the economic hardship for universities as a result of the impacts of the coronavirus pandemic, there will shortly be more opportunities for women, but they will have high – possibly invisible – risks. If you are offered an opportunity in the next short while, do your due diligence thoroughly and choose carefully and mindfully.

Some good stuff

There was a little bit of good news – sort of – from the 2020 WGEA report. In the agencies on which WGEA reports, the proportion of women in leadership roles increased. Specifically, the proportion of female CEOs increased from 17.1 percent to 18.3 percent, and female representation on boards increased from 26.8 percent to 28.1 percent. See why I said it was 'sort of' good news? These findings show a whopping 81.7 percent of CEOs in the group under WGEA's coverage are men, and 71.9 percent of board members in the same group are men. In universities, as I outlined in Chapter One, women are significantly under-represented in the professoriate and in the equivalent of CEO and board chair roles. As you may be beginning to tire of hearing, if you are a woman in academia in Australia, the odds are definitely against you.

But despite these odds, an increasing number and proportion of women are making it to the top in academia. Just today I heard of another female colleague being appointed to an executive director role at one of the universities I have worked at. She replaces a man. And last week, I saw a gender equity initiative at a different university I used to work at, where only female applicants are allowed for a senior executive and a second senior role. Whether this is because the university is embarrassed about its distinct lack of gender diversity, including a 100 percent all-male executive team, or the new vice-chancellor is enlightened and a really good bloke (I know him and he is both, actually) doesn't matter – meaningful action that will make a difference is being taken.

As well as the numbers and proportions changing, albeit slowly and only in small ways, awareness of the issue of sexist practices and decisions is growing in universities. I mentioned earlier that a small number of university executive teams have undertaken unconscious bias training. It would be great to see this in more – and every – university executive team and council across the country. Perhaps we will. As well as raising their own awareness of where they may have sexist views and thoughts and be making sexist decisions, senior university folk might then take action that will encourage you and other women to take steps you might not otherwise take. (Don't wait for this though – you might find yourself in the later stages of your career like me, still waiting for things to improve for women.)

Senior people need to be explicit about their disapproval of gender inequity in leadership.

In a newspaper article on gender discrimination at work, academic Adam Grant and Facebook COO Sheryl Sandberg discuss the matter of how to facilitate change[39]. They report that as a university professor, Grant thought that when he presented data on, and facilitated discussion around, women's underrepresentation in major leadership roles in his postgraduate classes, this would prompt action and change. It did not. When he repeated the exercise the following year, but added at the end in relation to female underrepresentation, 'I don't ever want to see this happen again', there was a whopping 65 percent increase in the number of female students who sought leadership roles that year compared to the previous year. The point Grant and Sandberg make is that senior people need to be explicit about their disapproval of gender inequity in leadership and also support females to step up and forward. If you have a leadership role (and I say more about this below), gently calling out your disapproval of gender imbalance this way and encouraging women to take steps to address it is likely to have a strong impact. Why not try it if the opportunity arises? Or ask a senior man to do so, pointing out the power he has in his words (he'll more than likely enjoy hearing this).

There is more that is good. You will know as a woman that female camaraderie is unique. When women get together, and there is female friendship and trust, there is nothing like it. We can trust (most) women. I have mentioned my all-female book group previously – outside work, the great pleasure and joy they add to my life helps make me the happy, productive professional I am at work. Most of the people with whom I have the closest and deepest connections at work are women, although there are some good blokes I know and work with too. But you can totally relax in the company of other women. You can share all of your experiences, fears, anxieties, joys and achievements as a woman with other women who can and will empathise, commiserate and celebrate with you.

One bad thing in amongst the good stuff

Although it's not good, I have to mention something I often get asked about when I speak about women and/or sexism publicly – the uncomfortable topic of women who don't support other women. There aren't many of these women who are not part of the sisterhood, but they do exist. You only have to be unlucky enough to work with one to know how potentially harmful and dangerous they can be to your wellbeing and your career. And I have observed that issues between women in the workplace are sometimes not taken as seriously as issues between men and women and those between men. Female relationship challenges, including bullying, can often be ignored, or dismissed as 'cattiness', which is, of course, another example of sexism.

I had the misfortune to report to one of these awful women for a time, and it was one of the worst periods of my professional life. She won awards for her alleged work supporting other women (no-one checked the evidence here, clearly) but the truth was that daily life under her was a living hell – for women and men. Narcissism is an abhorrent attribute of any leader but it feels especially repugnant in a female leader. But perhaps that's a sexist view – why should we expect a female leader to care for others any more than a male leader? In any case, I acknowledge that not all women are saints. I trust your radar will pick up the women who are self-absorbed, self-obsessed and self-centred and you will know to steer well clear.

Back to good stuff

There is also good in having to work harder (although we should not have to – but that's a 'should', which we have tried to banish for the purposes of this book). The good is that – if well managed – being challenged will promote your growth and development. By not being able to advance breezily and easily, you have the potential to become better and stronger because of your efforts to overcome the things holding you back. OK, I am clutching at 'good' straws here, I admit it.

Back to the less desperate good. The breakthroughs, when they happen for women, are wonderful. Given how much the odds are against us and how much sexism exists, when there is a leap forward of any kind – another female vice-chancellor is announced or a woman wins a large, competitive research

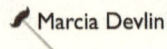
Marcia Devlin

grant as first chief investigator – we are individually and collectively joyous. Somehow because the wins are harder to achieve for women, the rewards are sweeter, and not only for the woman at the centre of the achievement, but for other women too.

More women are helping each other up

Another good phenomenon is, as the numbers of senior women grow, there are more of us to help women move up through the ranks. The reasons we help other women in their university career journeys might seem obvious. It often just comes naturally to those of us in a position to help. It's the right thing to do. Many of us may not even think about why we're doing it. Helping other women with their careers can come in the form of formal sponsoring, formal or informal mentoring or coaching, encouragement, acknowledgement, advice or suggestions, or even via a specific offer of assistance in some way. It can also come, often powerfully, from a simple, well-thought-out and well-timed compliment or series of compliments. The benefits of giving another woman a 'leg up' are numerous, and can have a far wider positive impact than just on the woman we might choose to help at that moment.

In addition to it being natural and the right thing to do, there are at least four other good reasons to support other women. The first is that it feels good! Research by psychologists, including Martin Seligman[40], has found that altruism and kindness to others is part of what creates genuine inner happiness. Others benefit from your help, and you feel good about that. That's a simple win-win situation right there.

The second reason is that the relationships that inevitably develop from helping each other are usually mutually beneficial. I certainly learn at least as much – and quite possibly more – from my mentees and the women I coach as I hope they learn from me. I find their perspectives insightful, their energy and enthusiasm inspiring, and their hope contagious. I always finish a mentoring or coaching session feeling energised.

Helping junior women might even create a connection that later pays off for a senior person in an unexpected way. This applies inside and outside one's career. I'll give you an example. When I was towards the end of a long and difficult labour with my first child, Finn, a midwife came on duty just before the birth. I was distressed by that point. We were about 24 hours into the labour (!) and Finn was comfortable where he was, thank you very much indeed. I was on my hands and knees on the floor of the shower. I was crying and feeling like I just could not go on and that no-one in the world cared (my husband was lying on a recliner chair, eating pizza, claiming he was 'tired and hungry after not eating for a day' – sheesh).

I was surprised to see the midwife who had just come on shift get down on her hands and knees, fully clothed, and crawl into the shower to be with me. She acknowledged how I was feeling, rubbed my back and told me what a great job I was doing. I noted she was wearing pantyhose under her uniform. I saw she still had her shoes on. I stared at her getting soaked there, on the floor, in front of me. I may have told her I loved her (OK, I did tell her I loved her). She made a huge difference to how I felt and to my ability to continue with the labour and see it through.

When she came to visit me and baby Finn the next day (a 28-hour labour, in case you're wondering), she told me she remembered me from several years previously. I looked at her. Nothing. She told me I had taught her in a transition to university study course. She told me she had often thought of me over the years and how kind I had been to her when she was a nervous new student transitioning to university study. She said she was so happy to recognise me when she came on shift that day and have the opportunity to return the favour during my labour of the kindness I had shown her years earlier as a student. In terms of career, you never know how helping a woman advance up the ladder might benefit your career or life at another point. One might not choose to help for that reason, but it can lead to an unexpected, positive outcome later.

Third, as I once heard Linda Burney MP say, acts of kindness and generosity inherent in helping other women are actually acts of leadership. You can demonstrate leadership through lending a hand to someone who needs it, or to someone who may not need it, but will benefit from it anyway. As well as making a positive contribution to the world, through such acts you also create trust and followers, two essential ingredients of effective leadership. We can all think of leaders who do not understand that leadership is not about them, it is about how they enable those in their care. When you think of a great leader you have worked with, you will no doubt think of someone who served others.

Finally, unless we pull other women up behind us, and even push them in front of us, we won't overcome the sexism that dogs us all. We won't be able to create positive change or progress for women in universities. I'm a really big advocate of senior women (and senior men) supporting women coming up behind us. It's one of the reasons I wrote this book. Without significant change in the gender balance of our university leadership teams, today's junior female academics and emerging female university leaders will

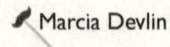
Marcia Devlin

still be facing sexism in yet another generation, and that will be to everyone's detriment. Gender balance change helps secure a better future for these women – the more women we support earlier in their career now, the more there will be in senior leadership positions in the future. Engaging in such support can also be a lot of fun and highly satisfying for you.

Why does it matter if there are fewer women in leadership in universities?

It is not fair that leadership opportunities are less often offered to women. Half the population are not getting a go. But I'm going to put aside the bleeding-heart arguments about what's fair, right and just and instead focus on the hard-nosed facts.

Based on research evidence, as I outlined earlier, Adam Grant and Sheryl Sandberg show:
- start-ups led by women are more likely to succeed than those led by men;
- innovative firms with more women in top management are more profitable; and
- companies with more gender diversity have more revenue, customers, market share and profits.

Jenny Hoobler and her colleagues conclude that the presence of a female CEO in an organisation is more likely to positively relate to the financial performance of the organisation[41].

In 2020, journalist Annabelle Crabb reported on a world-first study that shows a link between greater gender diversity and business success[42]. Specifically, the Australian study found that a female CEO increased market value by five percent – that's nearly $80 million to an average ASX200 company. The evidence shows that increasing the number of women in other key leadership positions by 10 percent or more increases a company's market value by 6.6 percent, or an average $105 million, according to Crabb. While universities aren't usually looking to make profits, they do need to be financially viable. The evidence suggests that, in the increasingly competitive, market-driven and accountable world in which universities operate, having women in the university leadership ranks will help their performance.

Taking that argument further, university councils who do not insist on gender-balanced boards and senior teams are doing their university a disservice. And, it could further be argued, such councils are not doing their jobs properly.

Are we there yet? Are we there yet?

When I was a child, we used to spend a bit of time in the car driving between Canberra – where we lived – and Sydney, where some close family friends who had emigrated from Ireland at about the same time as us lived. In those days, the trip took close to five hours. There was no such thing as in-built video entertainment in cars. Aircon and heating in cars either hadn't been invented or we couldn't afford it. Although it was always great to see our 'fake cousins' when we got to Sydney, the drive there always felt interminable. My sister and I used to ask our parents, over and over, 'Are we there yet? Are we there yet?' Eventually, my father banned the question, along with 'How much longer until we get there?' and every variation of the question we could think of. Sometimes, when I think about gender equity in universities, I feel like that child again.

While there is much that is good and changing for the better in gender equity in universities, the pace of change is slow. Things changed during my 30-year career in universities, but not so much that I can be confident yet that all will be well for the next generation of female leaders. For example, the same day I found out about the gender equity initiative I mention at the beginning of the chapter, I also found out that a talented senior female leader at the same university has decided to leave the university and possibly the sector. Two in, one out. But at least the gender initiative will add one woman to the currently all-male executive team at one university. And in early 2021, when I checked the publicly available information on university websites about the executive teams, this was not the only all-male executive in the country. Like those awfully long drives to Sydney, we still have much ground to cover.

Becoming a leader

You can help speed things up. There comes a point in a woman's journey in a university when you realise you are a leader. And you realise others see you that way. They are watching you and depending on you. For most of us, the realisation comes as a shock, and we feel like:
- there must be some mistake;
- I'm not ready to be a/the leader; and
- the real leader(s) will turn up soon.

Suck these feelings of inadequacy up, princess, because when this happens to you, your time has arrived – ready or not. Women are looking to

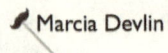
Marcia Devlin

you to lead them. That is how you know you've become a leader – not when you get a particular role or a particular title, not when you have a powerful position and women are wary of you, acutely aware you can use your power for good or for evil. When you realise women are looking to you, and up to you, regardless of your formal title, you are a leader. By the time you realise, chances are women will have been doing this for a while.

You might feel scared. You might have feelings of trepidation. These feelings are natural and normal. I had this realisation and these feelings when I realised I was a leader of women, and it was shocking to me. I wondered when the real grownups were going to arrive and take over and I could go back to being 'normal'. I couldn't and you can't. Don't worry, it's OK and life goes on. Actually it's a wonderful gift and privilege to be a leader. And particularly to be a leader of women. Embrace it.

Are women any good at leading?

My observations over decades indicate there are good and bad leaders in universities, regardless of gender. But perhaps because there are more male leaders and fewer female leaders, the women who make it up high often have outstanding leadership ability. A paper by Greg Young argues that successful leaders in the 21st century are able to respond to rapid change and to what the article describes as 'complex, wicked problems'[43]. Successful leaders, it claims, will be those who harness modern societal attitudes to ethics and fairness and embrace collaborative relationships. The paper argues that collaborative, rather than competitive, behaviour creates more success and, therefore, women – with their superior emotional intelligence and collaborative skills (his conclusions based on evidence) – are well placed to lead. The paper is about business leaders, but I agree with its arguments and they apply to female leaders in universities.

The paper reports on the findings of a study that employed a 360-degree assessment of the leadership ability of 161 leaders. The observed frequency of certain behaviours in leaders were compared with the desired frequency of the behaviours for a selection of emotional intelligence competencies relevant to effective leadership. In the study, women fared better in 15 of the 19 capabilities measured. These included empathy, the ability to be a skilful change catalyst, and being an inspirational leader, among others. This is only one study with a small sample size, but it is possible and entirely conceivable that women might be better than men at leading and more suitable for university top jobs than men. Whoops. No wonder some of the unenlightened men want to hold us back.

What about the men?

Where would we be without men in universities? (Um, we'd be in the professoriate and the executive team.)

Seriously, to beat the odds, we need the men. Men rule the world, including the universities. As I outlined in Chapter One, most of the Australian chancellors and vice-chancellors are men. In addition, most of the members of Australian executive teams are men. Well, I'm guessing this last claim is true as I haven't counted them recently. After three female executives who I happen to know made the difficult decision to step away from their executive roles in 2020, I didn't have the strength to check the most recent gender split in executive teams across the country. But the last official count in 2016 by *WomenCount*[44] revealed that men made up about two-thirds of executive team members in Australian universities. I'll bet my house they haven't improved significantly since 2016, and it's even possible they have got worse.

We need to work with the people who hold most of the power – the men.

So to help each other beat the odds, we need to work with the people who hold most of the power – the men. But working with them does not mean acquiescing to their gendered expectations of us. As I have explained throughout the book, it is up to us to start saying no to these expectations. The men may not like this, as it will disrupt what has been the natural order of things. As my mother would say to this, 'How sad, too bad, move on.'

My mother worked in a university for 40 years in professional staff roles. She started in the basement of the library sticking paper borrowing record slips inside the covers of books (remember those?). She rose to be head of academic appointments for the university, and she provided governance support for the senior appointment committees. She formally retired after 32 years but they kept bringing her back. For about eight years. Countless deans and heads of research centres and several vice-chancellors who passed through during her tenure had her on speed-dial. They would frequently and directly seek her view on appointments to contested senior roles. She often saw the value and potential of female candidates. She always honestly shared her opinion with the chair or panel member when they asked for it. She had a lot of influence – and therefore power – in her university. If you met her, you might not immediately see her power. She is tiny. She is friendly and engaging and, as she describes it, she 'chitter-chatters away' in a lovely Irish accent. But she became a trusted adviser of the most senior male officers of one university and frequently influenced their thinking. She worked effectively with the men.

I'm not as good at working with men as my mother was. I'm also tiny, and I try to be friendly and engaging (when I'm not busy giving someone one of my 'dirty looks' and being an Evil Overlady, obviously). Ironically, though, because I ended up in senior executive roles, I have had less power with the men than my mother had. As a senior executive officer of a university, you are expected to toe the line. You have less power than is widely assumed. While I have done as much as I can to help women advance, I have also watched women much further down the hierarchy have more influence than me because they use their ability to question things and call things out in ways I am not able to do. They skilfully use soft power and diplomacy to sway things. And they are sometimes listened to – perhaps at least partly because they are less threatening than a woman in senior leadership who is challenging gender stereotypes with her very existence.

What to do if you're a man

Quite a few enlightened men I have spoken to about this book have asked me whether there is a section for them. There is. Here it is.

Before I give you some suggestions, I want to say I appreciate you reading this book. I appreciate that you care about the sexism and related issues you see around you in universities. I appreciate that you are taking the time and making the effort to learn about the challenges and want to contribute to the solutions. Other women appreciate all of this too. We need you to help us address sexism. We need you to call out poor behaviour. We need you to help change the ways decisions are made. I don't have a playbook for you, but I offer a few suggestions below.

One behaviour you can help stop as a man, whatever your level or position in a university, is manterrupting. You can stop doing it yourself (you probably don't do it if you are reading this book, but just in case, I've included it). You can stop manterrupting and then saying, 'Sorry, I know I'm interrupting but...' and then finishing your interruption. You could help stop other men manterrupting. If a woman says, 'Dick, you just interrupted Jane', Dick is likely to continue as if the woman hasn't spoken. If you – as a man – say, 'Dick, you just interrupted Jane', Dick is likely to be momentarily confused and stop, at least briefly, before trying to continue manterrupting Jane. Say it again. Make Dick stop. See Jane continue. Take the rest of the day off.

The other obvious one you can specifically help with is stopping men bro-propriating women's ideas. All you need to say is, 'Great idea, Dave, that's exactly what Sophie said a few minutes ago.' Dave will look confused. Too bad. After the meeting, you could help Dave understand that he heard Sophie say the same thing, processed it, and then somehow believed he just thought of it on his own. Either that, or he wasn't listening when Sophie spoke, which is a bit rude. And sexist.

And a third idea is to explicitly support contributions that women make in meetings, particularly but not only if it is being ignored or, worse, dismissed. For example, you can back up ideas put forward by female colleagues. As a man, you are more likely to be listened to than your female colleagues are – that's our reality.

A fourth idea is to invite a woman to contribute to a discussion. You could use a preamble like, 'I know Fatima has done a lot of interesting work/research in this area, I'd really like to hear what she thinks about this proposal/plan/thing.' This way you both credential the female speaker and create a space for her to contribute. One thing I've noticed is as well as speaking more often in meetings (partly because they have most of the leadership roles), men take much longer turns than women when speaking. I'm sure there's research on this and a clever reader will let me know (thank you in anticipation) but just observe the next few meetings you attend and see for yourself. If you're a man and you want to make a useful contribution to sexism in universities, simply try to speak less often, for less time and try to listen more.

My intelligent, mindful, enlightened friend Brian read a draft of this book and asked whether there was scope to include a paragraph for men like him who didn't realise how bad the problem of sexism, discrimination and unconscious bias are. Brian added he felt that, to some extent, his parents and teachers had 'done a commendable job of conditioning' him to 'have a mindset that the sexes should be equal and women can expect to be able to pursue their ambitions on equal footing with men'. The problem, Brian added, is this 'should' was never followed up with a 'however, this is the way the world *actually is*', or, as Brian put it, with 'the truth' for women. Brian admitted he had – and probably still has – many blind spots in relation to these issues. He suggested this book might be useful for 'the ignorant, but essentially decent, blokes in terms of them waking up to the fact that there is a serious problem they can help with'.

Another specific action you can take that will help women is to demonstrably support your female colleagues in private. Brian told me

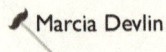
Marcia Devlin

one way he has had some success doing this in a male-dominated team is by politely making suggestions in one-to-one meetings with his (male) boss about how this boss could be using the particular skills and experience of one of the female team members to his best advantage. Brian specifically suggested this female staff member have the opportunity to present to senior people more often, which would make the male boss look good.

You may not like this one – and it's a repeat of an earlier comment – but it would be helpful if you stepped forward and did more of the office (and home) housework. I know you don't want to – neither do we – so splitting it 50/50 would be fair to us all. For example, next time you are in a kitchen, wash up the dishes in and around the sink, dry those dishes, find the places in the cupboard where those dishes go and put them back there and hang the tea towel up somewhere sensible to dry. Better still, if you're at work, bring a clean tea towel in from home and take the used tea towel home and wash and dry and fold it and bring it back. There is no Washing Up Fairy – women do most, if not all, of this sort of work.

Finally, please don't go this alone – the more men you can educate about sexism and how to eliminate it, the better off we will all be. And the less washing up you'll have to do at work.

The power to make change

We all have a role to play in making a change, even, and perhaps especially, if we are not men and not in formal positions of power. When I studied an executive short course at Stanford University in 2019, I learnt a little about power I didn't know before. For example, I learnt about social power. Social power comes from social networks and/or social capital – and not from powerful positions. It is an informal power. But the people who have it are often the real 'movers and shakers' within an organisation. I learnt these people gain their power by helping people, respecting others, being available and being perceived as having technical competence (or 'knowing things I need to know'). I learnt these people are perceived as intelligent and interpersonally competent – they are seen to have high IQ *and* high EQ.

Might you be, or become, one of these powerful people? And use your power to advance yourself and other women? I suspect my mother was powerful in her university because she was one of these socially powerful people. She 'chitter-chattered' away, building rapport and trust and while doing so she was also helping, respecting, being available and doing her job well. She was then able to influence decision-making in fundamental ways with the most senior men in the organisation. Could you do this too if you made it part of your advancement strategy? I know you could. You have a lot of power whether you know it or not. You need to work out how best to use it.

I also learnt there are at least seven personal qualities that build power: ambition, energy, focus, self-knowledge, confidence, empathy with others and a capacity to tolerate conflict. How do you rate on each of these? I'll bet it's highly on most, if not all, of them. You are a woman after all, and we are pretty damn fabulous. What are you going to do about gaining and using your power for your advancement and that of other women?

Is sexism ever useful?

There are times when the sexist views of women can be used to our benefit. These sexist views are permeating thinking and decisions every day. They're not going anywhere fast. So while you do all that is suggested in this book, you can also be aware of how you are viewed and how men in particular think about you – and consider using this to your advantage.

A young colleague who is an associate professor and strong researcher told me she approached her two male managers to negotiate an unusual remote-working arrangement (well before COVID-19, when working remotely was much more unusual than it is today). She prepared carefully for a meeting with each of them, where the matter would be discussed in detail. She communicated individually with each of the two managers in the lead up to her meetings. She outlined how the change she had proposed would increase her productivity and assist both the faculty and the university through her increased publications, profile and citations, as well as her future research grant success. In each meeting, the manager listened carefully to her carefully prepared arguments and evidence. In each meeting, the manager asked a similar question, along the lines of, 'Is that it? Are there any other reasons you want to set up this arrangement?'

In each meeting, at this point of the conversation, the manager brought up her family. When they did, my colleague commented that the arrangement would also better support her family and her ability to care for her three young children. In both cases, once she mentioned family and children, the male managers immediately agreed to the proposed arrangement. Despite the positive outcome, my colleague felt disappointed. She told me that although she got what she asked for, she wanted the decision and outcome to be based on her strengths, on merit and on the arguments about optimal productivity she had carefully prepared and put forward. She was disappointed the decision and outcome came through these men connecting her proposal with the traditional role of mother.

I say, 'Whatever it takes, within reason.' I was advised informally by human resources at one university that if I told my male line manager I needed time off, or flexibility, for family reasons, this would be well received by him and my request would be granted. They warned me that requesting the same for professional development reasons would not be well received and my request may not be approved. I lied to my manager the whole time I worked there and always got all I needed in terms of time away from the office and access to professional development opportunities. If he thought of me as a mother nurturing her children, rather than as a highly experienced, accomplished, internationally recognised, senior leader in higher education, I was prepared to go along with this – as long as I got what I needed professionally. What would have been the point of fighting this with a person so unenlightened that this was how he could be best influenced?

My young associate professor colleague's male line managers 'should' have been sold on her evidence-based arguments. My male line manager 'should' have let me go to seminars that would have helped me do my job better. No doubt. But we know about 'shoulds' and we have to decide what to 'do' in the meantime.

Using sexual harassment

At the beginning of the book, I told you it wasn't about sexual harassment or sexual assault. This next anecdote is about the former. So this is a trigger warning. It will be fine to skip over the story immediately below and pick up again at the next heading if you would prefer to do so.

There is a creepy senior male in one university I worked in who the women now call 'Mr Touchy-Feely'. He is in a high position of power. At a work event Mr Touchy-Feely, my husband and I attended, he pressed his palm in the small of my back and propelled me toward him while he leant in to kiss my cheek in greeting. I had just introduced him to, and was standing next to, my husband (so I was evidently not out to 'pick up' that night). At work, he used to touch me on the inner, upper arm. (By the way – for the avoidance of doubt – if you're a man reading this, it's not a good idea to touch women in the workplace, on any part of their body, for any reason, ever. Unless you have her expressed permission (and don't assume without asking and checking). Or you are keeping her alive with CPR until the ambulance arrives. I would have thought this was obvious and well understood, but Mr Touchy-Feely didn't seem to know or care about this obvious, accepted norm.)

When I shared the arm-touching story with a trusted female colleague, she told me she also had experiences with Mr Touchy-Feely. She explained that when she met up with him, he stood in front of her and held her by *both* inner upper arms at the same time. He then slid his two creepy hands down her arms, all the way to her wrists, which he then grabbed and used to propel her toward him so he could kiss her on both cheeks. Totally inappropriate. Totally gross. I asked her how she felt about his behaviour. She paused, looked at me and then laughed. This man had a lot of power over her career trajectory and success. She said, 'Whatever it takes, within reason, Marcia.'

We then both fell about laughing. Mr Touchy-Feely is completely revolting, but thinks he's Brad Pitt. He looks about 100 years old, give or take, and has bad breath. He's one of those men who is completely and utterly unaware of his male, pale, stale privilege and thinks he's got to the top on talent alone – and that he deserves to be there ahead of others. He takes himself extremely seriously. And he feels women up, dragging them toward him while inappropriately touching and kissing them, because he feels entitled and probably also partly because he thinks he's attractive. While his behaviour indicates deeply sexist views and is appalling, it is not unusual in a university – as many readers will know and you may even have experienced personally. And there are documented public cases we all know about.

The main point of the anecdote is that my senior colleague and I 'let' him do what he did (and later mocked and laughed at him privately) because this was the most helpful course of action to us at the time. We took the attitude of 'whatever it takes, within reason' in relation to tolerating his behaviour. It's an option with men. Because they rule the world, including the universities.

I don't advocate leaving sexual harassment unreported or 'letting' men harass you (that is, by not reporting it each and every time and possibly, thereby, leaving open the possibility for his interpretation that his behaviour is acceptable and that it may be repeated or escalated). My colleague and I were in positions where it would have significantly and negatively affected both of our careers to report this man's behaviour. The university was run as a boys' club where the men had each other's backs. Male vice-chancellor, male chancellor, mostly male executive – men, men, men everywhere. Big gender pay gap, defended as 'just the way things are'. An expectation that senior members of staff unquestioningly agree with the vice-chancellor, who is a deeply sexist man and oblivious to his sexism. At least one serious report of sexual harassment, where the woman stated her level of distress as extreme, went ignored for a period of time. We didn't stand a chance. But Mr Touchy-Feely will keep – and so will the written records of his behaviour my colleague and I have kept. And I might send him a copy of this book when it's

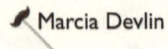

published with a blank sticky note marking this page and an arrow pointing to the rest of this sentence so he knows he's now on notice. In any case, COVID-19 has put paid to his creepy touchy-feelies, at least for now.

Things 'should' improve for women

Most of us think women's lots 'should' improve. There is little argument about that – in theory anyway. The problem is a lack of action. Like most of us, you may at times get stuck in the 'shoulds' – the university should do something, HR should do something, Mr Touchy-Feely should keep his hands to himself. Yes, they all should. But they aren't going to, or they aren't going to do enough, or they aren't going to act quickly enough to help you and your career. At least that's my prediction based on what's happened and not happened to date.

Right now, your advancement is up to you.

A word about humour

As you try to advance in academia, as well as doing what I have suggested in this book, consider trying to 'find the funny'. You might find this piece of advice unexpected. Hear me out.

Humour has multiple, positive effects. It encourages disrespect of something not worthy of respect – sexism in universities, for example. You can use humour to contribute to a culture of resistance to sexist expectations, challenge the absurdities of sexism, undermine the oppression women experience in universities and express dissent. You can also use humour to vent frustrations, lower your stress levels and preserve your sanity. It's worth thinking about.

Let me give you an example of my pursuit of humour. I follow a satirical Twitter account called @manwhohasitall. Essentially, it points out and mocks everyday sexism and gender stereotypes by simply switching the gender of questions normally asked and comments normally made about women. Examples include:

- MY DREAM: That one day boys will become anything they want to be: handsome princes, gentleman doctors, male rugby players and men chess players.
- ALL MEN! Is your hair weather-proof? Are your knees ready for Christmas? Are your legs neverending? Do your lips stay-put? Are you thin enough to be happy?

- TODAY'S DEBATE: To what extent are men who want their own careers selfish?
- ALL MEN! Just a little reminder to smile this evening, because women like to see positive men.
- TODAY'S FACT: Dads are doing the majority of home schooling, childcare and housework during lockdown because a) they enjoy it[,] b) they just happen to be better at it[,] and c) science.

If you're like me, you'll smile and sometimes laugh out loud while reading these – as well as cringing slightly as you are reminded that women are frequently offered ludicrous 'advice' and commentary such as in the list above.

You can apply gender reversal anywhere. For example, former Australian Prime Minister Julia Gillard writes in her recent book, *Women and Leadership*, co-authored with Ngozi Okonjo-Iweala, that there are at least 10 lessons to be learned from their interviews with female world leaders. My rough summary of the 10 are as follows:

1. Expect to be judged on your appearance (including clothes, hair and makeup) more than a man will be.
2. There is no right way to be a female leader but there will be expectations of you as a female leader that are specific to your gender.
3. You need to smile more as a woman to avoid having 'resting bitch face' (where a woman's neutral expressionless face is perceived as sour, hard, contemptuous and/or aggressive) and being seen as 'a bit of a bitch'.
4. Working through the arrangements for family with your partner will be necessary if you want to succeed.
5. Be careful about being pitted against other women.
6. Stick to your principles, especially when you are tempted not to do so.
7. Think about whether, how and when you will call out sexism against women.
8. Remember to role-model the positive as well as the challenges to encourage other women into leadership.
9. Network, network, network, and don't underestimate how much space you should take up.
10. Watch yourself – you might be falling into gendered stereotypes and highlighting your failings.

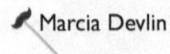
Marcia Devlin

Try reversing the gender in these pieces of advice from interviews with eight of the most powerful female world leaders. I found this exercise hilarious as it shows how absurd sexism is. And you know the saying, 'You have to laugh, or you'd cry.' This certainly applies to sexism in universities.

Beating the odds

As a woman, what can you do to beat the odds? I'm glad you asked. Here's a summary of what I recommend – that is, a summary of the advice in this book:

1. Review the data and facts – while we can argue about the 'why', the 'what' is undisputed – know the odds *are* against you advancing in academia.
2. Understand how sexism and gendered expectations of you are holding back your advancement.
3. Choose the attitudes you will adopt carefully – remember that being unladylike is dangerous as well as rewarding.
4. Prepare and implement a secret strategy. Focus on your personal values and professional priorities. Set goals, make plans, devise actions, then get to work.
5. Do more of what counts (showing off and research) and maximise, maximise, maximise. Do less of what doesn't count (housework) and say no more often.
6. Form a support squad and use them strategically at work and at home.
7. Decide what you are going to do about beating the odds, don a false moustache, then get to it.

Often, in the face of a seemingly overwhelming, large and entrenched problem, we can feel paralysed or just not know where to start. If you feel this way, start somewhere, start small and start where success is most likely. Chapter Three of this book is pretty easy going, for example, and will get you started with the careful thinking and decision-making necessary for your navigation.

If you wanted to stir things up a bit – and who would blame you – you could ask for gender-related information from your university. For example, you could write to the vice-chancellor and express your interest in gender equity. Ask him/her for data from the past five years on the number of men and women appointed to senior leadership or senior executive roles. Or you could write to the senior executive responsible for promotions (check the promotions policy to find out who this is) and ask for a comparison of the rates of promotion for men and women at your university over the past five years. You could write to the senior executive responsible for finance and/or human resources and ask about the gender pay gap at your university. It will be around 15 percent. Write back and thank them and ask why the gender pay gap exists and what is being done about it.

Just quietly, I would have loved it when I was senior deputy vice-chancellor and deputy chair of the gender equity committee at one university if requests and questions like these had been made and asked by women (or men) in the university. If they had been, we would have had to respond in some form and then possibly have been compelled to take some action to address the issues the questions uncovered.

As the James Brown song says, you've got the power*.

Conclusion

Circa 1990, when I was working in a university as a professional staff member and about to commence my academic career, there was an advertisement on television in Australia for Pantene shampoo. For whatever reason, it is well remembered by people alive at that time who had a television. A former model and celebrity from New Zealand called Rachel Hunter fronted the ad. In relation to one's hair becoming shinier (or was it bouncier?) from using the shampoo, Ms Hunter famously uttered the words, *'It won't happen overnight, but it will happen.'*

Because she is from New Zealand, she has that fabulous accent where the vowels are clipped. So, the words sounded (to Australians anyway) like, *'It won't hippen overnight, but it wull hippen.'* I still use this phrase frequently (complete with accent). I hear others use it too. Its enduring popularity comes partly from the fact that it contains a useful message. It suggests persistence, patience and not looking to quick fixes.

I would say the catchphrase is relevant to the careers of women in universities and similar organisations. If you know and acknowledge the odds, and do all I have suggested in this book, advancement *wull hippen*. But like shiny/bouncy hair, which takes multiple applications and a period of time to achieve, career advancement for women also takes effort and time.

I wish you all the best.

With your career *and* your hair, obviously.

What are you waiting for?

---

* I didn't put a reference in for this. It's on Spotify.

References

Chapter 1

1. Australian Government Department of Education, Skills and Employment (2020). Selected Higher Education Statistics – 2019 Staff data. Accessed October 10, 2020 from: https://docs.education.gov.au/node/53179
2. Jarboe, N. (2017). *WomenCount Australian Universities 2016*. WomenCount: UK. Accessed 10 October, 2020 from: https://womencountblog.wordpress.com/portfolio/womencount-australian-universities-2016/
3. Grant, A. and Sandberg, S. (2014). When talking about bias backfires. *The New York Times*. December 6, 2014. Accessed 10 October, 2020 from: https://www.nytimes.com/2014/12/07/opinion/sunday/adam-grant-and-sheryl-sandberg-on-discrimination-at-work.html
4. Cooper, S. (2018). *9 Non-Threatening Leadership Strategies for Women*. Accessed October 23, 2020 from: https://thecooperreview.com/non-threatening-leadership-strategies-for-women/

Chapter 2

5. Simmons, R. (2009). *The Curse of the Good Girl: Raising Authentic Girls with Courage and Confidence*. Penguin: New York.
6. Implicit Association Test. Accessed 11 November 2020 from: https://secure.understandingprejudice.org/iat/index2.htm. Note: this link is no longer available. There is a different test you could try at: https://implicit.harvard.edu/implicit/)
7. Sandberg, S. (2013). *Lean In: Women, Work and the Will to Lead*. WH Allen: UK.
8. McGinn, K. L. and Tempest, N. (2000, Revised 2010). *Heidi Roizen*. Harvard Business School Case, pp. 800-228.
9. Gillard, J. and Okonjo-Iweala, N. (2020). *Women and Leadership: Real Lives, Real Lessons*. Vintage: Australia.
10. MacNell, L., Driscoll, A., and Hunt, A. (2015). What's in a name: Exposing gender bias in student ratings of teaching. *Innovative Higher education, 40*(4). 291-303.
11. Clark, A. *University of Florida News*, 3 November, 2020. Accessed 11 November, 2002 from: https://news.ufl.edu/2020/11/ta-bias/
12. Garber, M. (2020). Kamala Harris's Ambition Trap. *The Atlantic*. November, 2020.
13. Grant, A. and Sandberg, S. (2014). When talking about bias backfires.

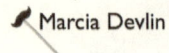

The New York Times. December 6, 2014. Accessed 10 October, 2020 from: https://www.nytimes.com/2014/12/07/opinion/sunday/adam-grant-and-sheryl-sandberg-on-discrimination-at-work.html

Grant and Sandberg refer to the following three studies:

1. Dezsö, C. and Gadis Ross, D. (2012). Does female representation in top management improve firm performance? A panel data investigation. *Strategic Management Journal, 33*(9), 1072-1089.
2. Herring, C. (2009). Does Diversity Pay?: Race, Gender, and the Business Case for Diversity. *American Sociological Review, 74*(2), 208-224.
3. Paustian-Underdahl, S. C., Walker, L. S., and Woehr, D. J. (2014). Gender and perceptions of leadership effectiveness: A meta-analysis of contextual moderators. *Journal of Applied Psychology, 99*(6), 1129–1145.

14 Crabb, A. (2019, September) Men at Work: Australia's Parenthood Trap. *Quarterly Essay 75*. Black Inc books: Melbourne

15 Williams, J. and Dempsey, R. (2014). *What Works for Women at Work: Four Patterns Working Women Need to Know.* NYU Press: New York.

16 Reilly, N. (2019). Why must women leaders learn 'gender judo' to stay likeable at work? *The Sydney Morning Herald.* Accessed 11 November 2020 from https://www.smh.com.au/lifestyle/life-and-relationships/why-must-women-leaders-learn-gender-judo-to-stay-likeable-at-work-20190904-p52nzj.html

Chapter 3

17 Seligman, M. (1972). *Learned Helplessness.* Accessed December 11, 2020 from: https://www.annualreviews.org/doi/pdf/10.1146/annurev.me.23.020172.002203

18 ABC television (2020, November 9) Inside the Canberra Bubble. *Four Corners.* Accessed November 30, 2020 from: https://www.abc.net.au/4corners/inside-the-canberra-bubble/12864676

19 Bennett, J. (2015). How not to be 'manterrupted' in meetings. *The New York Times* (January 15, 2015). Accessed March 21, 2021 from: https://time.com/3666135/sheryl-sandberg-talking-while-female-manterruptions/

20 MacNell, L., Driscoll, A., and Hunt, A. (2015). What's in a name: Exposing gender bias in student ratings of teaching. *Innovative Higher education, 40*(4), 291-303.

21 World Economic Forum (2019). *Mind the 100 Year Gap.* Accessed November 30, 2020 from: https://www.weforum.org/reports/gender-gap-2020-report-100-years-pay-equality

22 Grant, A. and Sandberg, S. (2015). Madam C.E.O., Get me a coffee. *The New York Times.* (February 8, 2015). Accessed October 8, 2020 from: https://www.nytimes.com/2015/02/08/opinion/sunday/sheryl-sandberg-and-adam-grant-on-women-doing-office-housework.html

Chapter 4

23 The Seven Fs. Accessed December 3, 2020 from: https://www.goodleadership.com/seven-fs/
24 World Economic Forum (2019). *Mind the 100 Year Gap*. Accessed November 30, 2020 from: https://www.weforum.org/reports/gender-gap-2020-report-100-years-pay-equality
25 Tuglan, B. (2020). Learn when to say no. *Harvard Business Review*. September-October, 2020). Accessed Decemebr 11 from: https://hbr.org/2020/09/learn-when-to-say-no
26 Heijstra, Thamar M.; Einarsdóttir, Þorgerður; Pétursdóttir, Gyða M.; Steinþórsdóttir, Finnborg S. (2017). Testing the concept of academic housework in a European setting: Part of academic career-making or gendered barrier to the top? *European Educational Research Journal, 16*(2-3), 200-214.
27 Macfarlane, B. and Burg, D. (2019). Women professors and the academic housework trap. *Journal of Higher Education Policy and Management, 41*(3), 262-274.
28 Grant, A. and Sandberg, S. (2015). Madam C.E.O., Get me a coffee. *The New York Times*. (February 8, 2015). Accessed October 8, 2020 from: https://www.nytimes.com/2015/02/08/opinion/sunday/sheryl-sandberg-and-adam-grant-on-women-doing-office-housework.html

Chapter 5

29 Sadler, D.R. (1999). *Managing your Academic Career: Strategies for Success*. The University of Queensland. Accessed 18 November, 2020 from: https://www.researchgate.net/publication/318543954_Managing_your_Academic_Career_Strategies_for_Success
30 Bradberry, T. (2016). Critical Things Ridiculously Successful People Do Every Day. LinkedIn. Accessed December 11, 2020 from: https://www.linkedin.com/pulse/critical-things-ridiculously-successful-people-do-every-bradberry/
31 Francisco, D. (2015, January). How to be the CEO (Chief Energy Officer). Presentation to Victorian Employers' Chamber of Commerce and Industry (VECCI). Melbourne.
32 Maushart, S. (2003). *Wifework: What Marriage Really Means for Women*. Bloomsbury: USA.

Chapter 6

33 de Vries, J., & Binns, J. (2018). Sponsorship: Creating Career Opportunities for Women in Higher Education. Accessed 11 December, 2020 from: https://www.universitiesaustralia.edu.au/wp-content/uploads/2019/06/UAEW-Sponsorship-Guide.pdf

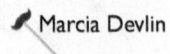

34 Gillard, J. and Okonjo-Iweala, N. (2020). *Women and Leadership: Real Lives, Real Lessons*. Vintage: Australia.

35 Maushart, S. (1997). *The Mask of Motherhood: How Becoming a Mother Changes Everything and Why We Pretend it Doesn't.* Random House Australia.

Chapter 7

36 World Economic Forum (2019). *Mind the 100 Year Gap*. Accessed November 30, 2020 from: https://www.weforum.org/reports/gender-gap-2020-report-100-years-pay-equality

37 Workplace Gender Equality Agency (2020, November). *Australia's Gender Equality Scorecard*. Accessed November 30, 2020 from: https://www.wgea.gov.au/sites/default/files/documents/2019-20%20Gender%20Equality%20Scorecard_FINAL.pdf

38 Ryan, M. K. and Haslam, S.A. (2005). The glass cliff: Evidence that women are over-represented in precarious leadership positions. *British Journal of Management, 16*, 81-90.

39 Grant, A. and Sandberg, S. (2014). When talking about bias backfires. *The New York Times*. December 6, 2014. Accessed 10 October, 2020 from: https://www.nytimes.com/2014/12/07/opinion/sunday/adam-grant-and-sheryl-sandberg-on-discrimination-at-work.html

40 Seligman, M. (2002). *Pursuit of Happiness*. Accessed 11 November 2020 from: https://www.pursuit-of-happiness.org/history-of-happiness/martin-seligman-psychology/

41 Hoobler, J. M., Masterson, C. R., Nkomo, S. M., and Michel, E. J. (2016). *The business case for women leaders: Meta-analysis, research critique, and path forward*. Paper presented at Closing the Gender Gap: Advancing Leadership and Organizations. DOI: 10.5703/1288284316077

42 Crabb, A. (2020, June 19). World first research shows female CEOs boost companies by $80 million on average. *ABC News*. Accessed November 5, 2020 from: https://www.abc.net.au/news/2020-06-19/women-in-leadership-boost-success/12370516?utm_source=abc_news&utm_medium=content_shared&utm_content=mail&utm_campaign=abc_news

43 Young, G. (2016). Women, Naturally Better Leaders for the 21st Century. Whitepaper. Routledge. Accessed December 11, 2020 from: https://www.routledge.com/rsc/downloads/WP-TL2-2016_Transpersonal_Leadership_WP2_FINAL.pdf

44 Jarboe, N. (2017). *WomenCount Australian Universities 2016*. WomenCount: UK. Accessed 10 October, 2020 from: https://womencountblog.wordpress.com/portfolio/womencount-australian-universities-2016/

Acknowledgements

This book sort of came about by accident when I – yet again – failed to get a job. I had applied to work with Julia Gillard in her Global Institute for Women's Leadership. While my application was not successful, the reflection that formed part of the application process led me to two realisations. The first was that after 30 years of experiencing sexism in universities as a woman, I needed some therapy. Writing a book on the topic has provided the necessary therapy. The second was that after supporting, mentoring and coaching hundreds, if not thousands, of women over decades in the sector, a summary of what I had learned would be a useful way to meet my professional goal of helping as many women as possible. This book is that summary. So I'd like to thank Julia Gillard for rejecting me. (P.S. You might be relieved to know that a bloke did not get the job.)

I have been thinking about and developing some of the ideas in this book for years. Earlier and/or shorter versions – or fragments of – sections of this book have appeared in my columns in *The Age* and articles in *Women's Agenda* and *SmartCompany* as well as in LinkedIn articles and posts. I would like to thank the many editors I had at *The Age* over the 22 years I wrote for Fairfax Media. I'd particularly like to thank Julie Hare, who published my articles in *Campus Review* and *The Australian* for many years for all she taught me about the craft and 'tapestry' of writing.

I have started several sole-authored books, and the numerous unfinished manuscripts now take up much valuable space on my computer hard drive. I'm a big fan of coaches and coaching, so I took my own advice on the value of both and employed a book coach to help me write this book. I know – I'd never heard of a book coach either. Turns out, they are pretty cool. I'd like to thank Kath Walters for her guidance, mentoring, structure, direction, redirection, facilitation and feedback. I highly recommend Kath's services.

Thank you to the almost 12,000 people on LinkedIn who read an early post about this book, the scores who commented on that post and contacted me and all of those who pre-ordered copies – your interest has sustained me. Thank you to: Catherine Lovelock for asking the right questions; Niki Kolouris for persuading me to try new ways of writing; Emeritus Professor Lorraine Ling for decades of mentoring and for reading an early draft and offering feedback; Dr Juliana Ryan for the laughs and the early read and feedback; Associate Professor Zali Yager for reminding me about what was important; Associate Professor Camilla Brockett who urged me on (and gave me a keep-cup); Associate Professor Kathy Tangalakis who asked me to mentor her, from whom I have learned a lot and who was pivotal in my decision to write this book; Associate Professor Nina Fotinatos for her years of support; The White Jacket Group for helping me see I had valuable advice to offer; Ellen Sabo for her encouragement; Dr Meg Elkins for the stories I didn't use but that provided the anger I needed to fuel me at times; my book group members, Meg, Chris, other Chris, Mia, Sharon, Fi and Clare (yes I will appear as a guest writer at a book group, thank you for asking); Professor Sarah O'Shea for the early read and feedback, the craic and the reassurance; Brian Martin, who helped with the men's bits; Dr Joanne Pyke for her time and wisdom; Professor Sally Kift for somehow making time to read a draft; Dr Jade McKay for her longstanding partnership and encouragement; Jaimee Westin for advice on design; Jess Horton for early editing; and Claire McGregor for later editing and proofreading, the book design and layout and the fabulous cover.

Thank you to my parents, Angela and Barney Devlin, for teaching me not to suffer fools gladly, or in any other way for that matter. Thanks to Dad for role-modelling the discipline and joy of writing. He wrote in his journal every day for decades – from the 1960s right up until days before his death in 2018. He also wrote and published witty, educational and entertaining plays that have been performed in Australia and Ireland, in English and in Irish. Thanks to Mum for teaching me the power of kindness, the joy of giving to others and not to put up with charlatans.

To my two favourite sons – Finn and Aengus – thank you for being delightful human beings and making your father and I think we had a tiny bit to do with it. Thanks especially to Finn for his marketing and promotion strategy advice and Aengus for help with restraint – including by giving me 'the look' when I suggested a number of potential (ridiculous) inclusions in this book.

Finally, I'd like to thank Pete – my husband, partner, father of our children and the single most influential positive factor in my career success over three decades. Everything I have done since I met him has been enhanced by his contributions.

About the Author

An academic since 1991, a professor since 2008, senior university executive since 2012, and now a global thought leader in education and equity, Marcia Devlin has plenty of experience as a woman beating the odds.

An accomplished academic, with colleagues she has won over $6 million in competitive, commissioned and other funds and has led numerous national research projects on education and equity. Internationally recognised for her expertise in these areas, she has been invited to give over 100 headline addresses in 10 countries. Based on her body of research work, Marcia is an elected Lifelong Fellow of the UK-based Society for Research in Higher Education (SRHE).

An award-winning writer, Marcia has over 320 publications comprising academic, professional and media outputs. She was a regular contributor and columnist for Fairfax Media for over 20 years, wrote for the Murdoch Press for more than a decade and has been writing for APN Educational Media since 2003. Marcia has also been published by *The Conversation, SmartCompany, Women's Agenda* as well as numerous academic publishers. She writes a regular column for the Higher Education Research and Development Society of Australasia's *HERDSA Connect*, read across Australia, New Zealand and parts of Asia, and the UK-based *SRHE News* and *SRHE Blog*, read in 117 countries. Her research and commentary work are widely read and cited across the world.

Marcia is a strong and vocal advocate for women. She has mentored, coached and/or directly and indirectly supported hundreds, if not thousands, of women seeking to progress and advance in their careers. She has created and introduced university-wide programs to mentor women at scale and to provide peer support and development. She has personally supported numerous women to win awards – for their teaching, their leadership, their policy-making and their administration. Marcia served as elected co-leader of the Universities Australia Executive Women initiative, co-commissioning practical guides to help universities recruit more senior women and to sponsor women's career advancement.

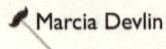
Marcia Devlin

Women have told Marcia she has inspired them to ask for raises, say no to unfair requests, query decisions that negatively affect their career, make enquiries about pay gaps, challenge biases, negotiate higher salaries, change jobs, support their daughters in their ambitions, enrol in further qualifications to improve their career options and to improve their sense of worth and self-esteem. She has written this book to augment those contributions.

Marcia lives in Melbourne with her husband and near her two favourite sons.

www.ingramcontent.com/pod-product-compliance
Lightning Source LLC
Chambersburg PA
CBHW021950290426
44108CB00012B/1013